Ambrose Tighe

**The Development of the Roman Constitution**

Ambrose Tighe

**The Development of the Roman Constitution**

ISBN/EAN: 9783744771108

Printed in Europe, USA, Canada, Australia, Japan

Cover: Foto ©ninafisch / pixelio.de

More available books at **www.hansebooks.com**

*History Primers.*

# THE DEVELOPMENT

OF THE

# ROMAN CONSTITUTION

BY

AMBROSE TIGHE

FORMERLY TUTOR AND DOUGLAS FELLOW AT YALE COLLEGE

NEW YORK
D. APPLETON AND COMPANY
1889

# PREFACE.

DURING my tutorship at Yale College, I offered several courses, all of which had more or less to do with Roman history. Roman history divides itself quite naturally into three periods, the first of which extends to the conclusion of the second Punic war. In this early time the evidence is largely philological. Any intelligent criticism of it is, therefore, impossible without some knowledge of how language lives and grows. The root, the stem, the termination, and the derivation, which are so incomprehensible to the Philistine, have here the greatest importance. For this reason, in one of my courses, an attempt was made to fix the position of the Latin language by some discussion of the nature of language, the relation of languages, and the principles of euphony, and by applying these general ideas to Latin word-formation, etymology, and syntax. After reasonable opportunities in this direction, I took it that one would be ready to learn something about the development of the Roman state, and of its political, legal, and religious institutions. This is a very large subject, and, in the few weeks which I had at my command, a simple line of thought only could be followed. With a view to economizing time and effort, I prepared for the use of my classes a series of tracts on leading points in the history of the period covered. The idea was not original, but had been employed before with much success by Mr. E. D. Robbins, a former incumbent of the position which I held. As resorted to by myself, this method of instruction was by no means an exclusive one. Wherever it seemed more profitable for the student to cover the ground in another way it was followed. Where there was no complexity or great continuity of thought, and the chief importance attached to the illustrations, the lecture was found the most economical medium of instruction. On other points there was accessible much material in standard books of reference in the possession of the student. And in general, in what I printed, I aimed simply to give an outline of the matter treated, relying on the familiar class-room devices to give color and accuracy to the picture. The following pages are these tracts in a somewhat revised form.

I have thought it worth while to give thus, at length, the history of this book's composition, because its possibilities and its limitations are in this way suggested. I used to, perhaps, delude myself with the thought that some of the men who took my courses got a better and more scientific notion of why Rome was great from the use of my tracts than they would have from a dictionary of Roman antiquities. This was partly because the omission of details made it easy to follow the thread of development, and to see the general in the particular; and because, in the second place, it was possible to constantly call their attention to the nature of the evidence in support of the positions successively taken. The ideal text-book in Roman history will be one which, in one part, will give a conservative statement of what some prominent scholar takes to be true, and in its notes will collate all intelligent views which are in conflict with this, and perhaps weigh their claims to consideration. In what I have written, I have followed Mommsen very closely wherever he throws any light at all on the subjects discussed. I have done this in some cases in spite of my own conviction that he is in error. In one or two instances where this has been so, I have hinted at the better opinion. Thus, for example, in the second chapter, on the structure of ancient society, I have no faith at all in the historical accuracy of the notion that the *gens* was a union of kinsmen. I am myself a disciple of the anthropological school, so far as any such school exists. But in view of the fact that Mommsen seems to sympathize with the other theory, and of the general uncertainty on the question, I considered it too radical a course to give the chief prominence to its creed, although I feel it to be the more reasonable one, and have contented myself with referring to its existence. In the same way I have excepted to Mommsen's idea as to the primitive constitution of the *comitia centuriata*. Where, on the other hand, I have found myself in doubt among conflicting views, I have adopted Mommsen's outright. Thus I think that the unprejudiced student, after reading Mommsen's argument for the existence of the *concilium tributum plebis*,* will be inclined to enter a verdict of "not proven." But I have accepted it simply on the basis of authority.

I should approach nearer to my ideal, if, in addition to thus attempting to follow one authority, I had added at least the bibliography which I gave to my classes as a guide to the best which had been said and thought on the general subject. This, however, would swell the size of the volume beyond the primer limit, as well as be the least bit presumptuous, in as far as it would attempt to call the attention of the teaching profession to a list of authorities, the evidence of whose use they will readily recognize when they examine what I have written. I have felt quite free in drawing on every ac-

* "Forschungen."

cessible source of information, and my book is nothing more than a compilation. Some parts are obvious translations of Mommsen and Lange, and even some have been made up from contemporary literature of the kind which appears in the magazines. I have received the greatest help in what I have said of the Roman religion from an admirable article by Professor W. F. Allen on "The Religion of the Ancient Romans," in Volume CXIII of the "North American Review." The line of thought in reference to the early commercial greatness of Rome was suggested by an essay of Goldwin Smith's, from which I have borrowed without stint, and, not to carry this enumeration too far, every one who reads my first chapter will see how I am indebted there to the introduction to J. R. Seeley's edition of Livy's first book.

If the volume were ambitious enough to support a dedication, I should inscribe it to the five hundred young men who in one course or another studied Roman history with me at Yale College. I found in them in full measure the qualities which make men pleasant companions and human intercourse a delight. They were courteous, generous, appreciative, intelligent, and enthusiastic. It was a great privilege to meet them as I did, and my recollections of them are of the happiest nature.

ST. PAUL, MINNESOTA, *June, 1886.*

# CONTENTS.

## CHAPTER I.

### THE SOURCES OF EARLY ROMAN HISTORY.

|  | PAGE |
|---|---|
| The Credibility of Early Roman History | 7 |
| These Reasons for Skepticism explained | 8 |
| The Historians and Annalists of Early Rome | 10 |
| The Sources of the Legendary History of Rome | 11 |
| Etiological Myths | 12 |
| The Teachings of Euhemerus | 14 |
| The Contribution of Deliberate Invention | 15 |
| Can we know anything, then, about Early Roman History? | 17 |
| How the Science of Language helps us | 18 |
| Etymological Evidence | 20 |
| The Contribution of Comparative Law | 22 |
| Inferences from the Later History of the City | 24 |
| What we can learn from these Sources | 25 |

## CHAPTER II.

### THE STRUCTURE OF ANCIENT SOCIETY.

|  | |
|---|---|
| The Roman Family | 28 |
| The Beginnings of Rome | 29 |

|                                                                 | PAGE |
| --------------------------------------------------------------- | ---- |
| What was a Clan?                                                | 31   |
| The Patriarchal Theory                                          | 32   |
| The Application of these Criticisms to Roman History            | 34   |
| The Early Roman Religion                                        | 35   |
| The Early Romans' Ideas about the Dead                          | 38   |
| The Influence of these Beliefs within the Family                | 40   |
| The Influence of these Beliefs without the Family               | 41   |
| The City of Rome                                                | 42   |

## CHAPTER III.

### ROME UNDER THE KINGS.

|                                                            |    |
| ---------------------------------------------------------- | -- |
| The Power of the King                                      | 44 |
| Restrictions on the King's Power                           | 45 |
| The Comitia Curiata                                        | 47 |
| The Functions of the Comitia Curiata                       | 49 |
| The Senate and its Functions                               | 49 |
| The Early Greatness of Rome                                | 51 |
| The Evidences of this Early Commercial Greatness           | 52 |
| The Plebeians                                              | 54 |
| The Primitive Political Condition of the Plebeians         | 57 |

## CHAPTER IV.

### THE EARLIEST REFORMS IN THE ROMAN CONSTITUTION.

|                                                                       |    |
| --------------------------------------------------------------------- | -- |
| Ths Burdens of Citizenship                                            | 59 |
| The Servian Classification                                            | 60 |
| How the Exercitus of Servius became the Comitia Centuriata            | 62 |
| The Establishment of the Consular Government                          | 63 |
| The Dictator and the Quæstors                                         | 65 |
| What the Plebeians gained by these Changes                            | 66 |

## CHAPTER V.

### THE FIGHT WITHOUT THE CITY.

|  | PAGE |
|---|---|
| The Non-Italian Races of Italy | 68 |
| The Italian Races of Italy | 69 |
| The Latin League | 70 |
| The Conquest of Italy | 71 |
| The Greatness of Rome | 74 |
| What Rome learned in these Wars | 76 |
| The Policy of Incorporation | 78 |
| The Subject Communities of Italy | 80 |
| Rome's Colonial System | 82 |
| The Roman Roads | 83 |

## CHAPTER VI.

### THE FIGHT WITHIN THE CITY.

| | |
|---|---|
| Primitive Ideas about Property | 85 |
| The Land System of the Romans | 86 |
| The Lands acquired in War | 87 |
| The State's Lands under the Consular Government | 88 |
| The Early Agrarian Troubles | 90 |
| The Tribunes of the Plebs | 91 |
| The Concilium Tributum Plebis | 92 |
| How the Tribuneship worked in Practice | 94 |
| The Decemvirate | 95 |
| The Influence of the Decemvirate's Legislation on the Development of Roman Law | 96 |
| The Political Effect of the Decemvirate's Legislation | 98 |
| The Consular Tribunes | 100 |
| The Military Quæstor, the Censor, the Prætor, and the Curule Ædile | 101 |

|  | PAGE |
|---|---|
| The Greater Gods of the Romans | 102 |
| The Greek Modifications of the Roman Religion | 105 |
| The Value of this Transformation | 106 |
| The Priesthoods | 108 |
| The End of the Struggle | 110 |
| The Economic Results of the Struggle | 111 |
| The Social Results of the Struggle | 112 |

## CHAPTER VII.

### HOW ROME WAS GOVERNED AT THE TIME OF THE SECOND PUNIC WAR.

| | |
|---|---|
| The Nobilitas | 114 |
| The Constitution of the Senate | 115 |
| The Theoretical Functions of the Senate | 117 |
| The Popular Assemblies enumerated | 118 |
| The Composition of a Tribe | 119 |
| The Censors' Control over the Tribes | 120 |
| The Theoretical Powers of the Popular Assemblies | 122 |
| The Magistrates' Control over the Popular Assemblies | 123 |
| The Senate's Control over the Magistrates | 125 |
| The Senate's Executive Power | 127 |
| The Rule of the Nobilitas | 128 |
| The Transition to the Empire | 130 |

# THE DEVELOPMENT

OF THE

# ROMAN CONSTITUTION.

---

## CHAPTER I.

### THE SOURCES OF EARLY ROMAN HISTORY.

1. **The Credibility of Early Roman History.**—No one in these days, who has studied the subject with any care, believes that the stories about the kings and early heroes of Rome are quite true in the form in which we have received them from the Greek and Latin writers. Some scholars dispose of them curtly as a mass of fables, unworthy of serious study. Others think that, if they be analyzed and sifted, some truth can be found in them amid much which is false. A few divide them into two parts—the larger one made up of facts and the smaller of fictions. But no one, as we have said, accepts them as a whole without question. This general skepticism, however, dates no further back than the early part of the present century. Then, under the influence of a German scholar, Niebuhr by name, the scientific criticism of Roman history first began. Before this time Romulus and his six successors on the Roman throne were no more

mythical in the general view than any seven mediæval sovereigns of France or England, and Servius Tullius was as historical a statesman as Oliver Cromwell or Cardinal Richelieu. But, since there has been direct and dispassionate inquiry into the character and authority of these stories, it has been made very clear that many of them at any rate ought not to be regarded in the same light as events of more recent times, and this for several reasons. One reason is, that they tell largely of things which are very improbable because inconsistent with what we have good grounds for regarding as laws of nature. Another is, that even these improbable stories destroy themselves by their inconsistencies and contradictions. And a third is, that they are unsupported by any contemporary evidence.

2. **These Reasons for Skepticism explained.**—Of course, there would be no sufficient ground for the rejection of any particular legend if skepticism in regard to it were based on any one of these reasons alone. It is only when we find two or more of them uniting to undermine our belief, that we are justified in yielding to them. For example, we can not with accuracy say that any event is intrinsically impossible. The great majority of people in the world will accept on sufficient evidence any consistent story, no matter how contrary it is to their own experience. Or, again, if a story is reasonable and well vouched for, an inconsistency or two in it can be explained away or passed over. Or, finally, a reasonable, consistent, and uncontradicted story, which could be handed

down by word of mouth, does not need written testimony to secure for it a hearing with fair-minded men. To make a specific application of these principles, it is, to say the least, very unlikely that the city of Rome was built in the year 753 B. C. by two brothers, Romulus and Remus, who, though the sons of a god, were nursed by a wolf. The intrinsic difficulties of such a tale would seem sufficient to destroy it. Cities, according to general human experience, are not built, but grow—and that, too, not by the work of one or two men in a short time, but during the course of many years and gradually. But, on the other hand, however unusual it may be for sons of gods to be nursed by wolves and to become the founders of cities, here may have been an exception to all the ordinary presumptions, and, if the story be uncontradicted and well authenticated, we may take it as an exception. But, in point of fact, we have received from the ancients twenty-four other accounts of the founding of Rome, which are wholly inconsistent with this, the best known one, and with each other. What, then, shall we do? Shall we reject them all? No, it may be answered; we should accept that which rests on the best evidence. But, as we shall presently show, there is no evidence which is worth anything for any of them. This, then, is a legend, unreasonable *a priori*, and contradicted by more than a score of others, which are equally well supported, but for all of which, at the same time, there is no support of any value. Stories of such sort, it will be readily granted, are not worthy of belief.

3. **The Historians and Annalists of Early Rome.**—When we question in this way the evidence on which all these tales are based, we imply that we attach but little importance to the testimony of the ancient authors about this early period, but we think that a brief consideration will make it quite clear that we are justified in this. We get our knowledge of the legendary history of Rome chiefly from Livy and Dionysius of Halicarnassus. Other ancient writers, however, supplement in one way or another what they tell us. The anecdotes of Plutarch, for example, give interest and color to the record of this as well as of a later time. Livy wrote in Latin and Dionysius in Greek, and both lived during the reign of the Emperor Augustus, seven hundred years after the legendary founding of the city, and nearly five hundred after the expulsion of the kings. Neither of them could, therefore, have had any original knowledge of events as remote as these, but they must have derived their information from previous writers whose works are not accessible to us. These previous writers of history are grouped together under the general name of annalists, and the earliest of them, Quintus Fabius Pictor and Lucius Cincius Alimentus, were contemporaries of the second Punic war (218 B. C.). They seem to have written condensed and colorless accounts of the times before their own, and then to have followed these with detailed and full records of things which they themselves had seen or of which they had learned from their fathers. They afforded, therefore, for the use of the later his-

torians, complete and, on the whole, reliable material, beginning perhaps with the time of Pyrrhus (280 B.C.). But about the regal period, which ended three hundred years before the earliest of them wrote, they in turn could have had no original knowledge. If there were no contemporary historians for these first five hundred years of the city, as seems to have been the case, how did the annalists learn about what happened during them?

4. **The Sources of the Legendary History of Rome.**—We can answer this question by saying that they must have relied mainly on oral tradition. For the regal period there was hardly any other source of information open to them. For the next two centuries there was enough to fix the chronology, if they had the patience to consult it, but the details must in any event have been supplied from nothing more trustworthy than common report, or have been invented by the historian. To fix the chronology certain public and private records were available, concerning which we know more or less. For one thing there were (1) the *Fasti*. These were chronological lists of the public magistrates, and seem to have extended as far back as the beginning of the republic. Second, there were (2) certain inscriptions on brass or stone, preserving treaties or laws. Third, (3) in some books of ancient religious or civil procedure, material for history could incidentally be found. Fourth, there were the (4) *Annales Maximi*, which were brief records made annually by the *pontifex maximus*, who in this way kept alive the memory of things

which seemed to him important, such as plagues, eclipses, and other phenomena of nature, the price of grain, and the like. Those covering the years previous to 390 B. C., however, appear to have perished in the burning of the city by the Gauls. Finally, noble families, whose members had done great things in the state, had memoranda of these achievements in their possession. Under the images of their ancestors, which hung in the *atria* of their houses, were brief biographical inscriptions, and somewhere perhaps in the third century before Christ, it became the custom to commit to writing, for the guidance of future orators, at least an outline of the funeral eulogies which were delivered over the noble dead. When we have enumerated these, we have told of practically all the written material which Fabius Pictor and his successors had at their command for the composition of the history of the times before their own. If we can conceive of them as exercising the care and diligence of a modern historian in their work, they could not have extracted from all these sources more than a thin thread of events, running back with diminishing strength to the beginning of the republic and stopping there. This shows that what they and those who draw from them give us need not detain us long.

5. **Etiological Myths.**—But modern criticism goes still further than this, and undertakes to point out the origin of these impossible, contradictory, and unauthenticated stories. It suggests how many of them may have come into existence;

and, even if we refuse to allow the validity of its conjectures in a single instance, we shall at any rate see, from still another point of view, how uncertain and assailable is the material which we are considering. There is a tendency, then, to regard the forms of these legends which we have, as survivals from various versions which were current among the Romans themselves, and which originated in some one of several ways. One class is taken to be etiological (*cf. αἰτία,* "a cause") in its character. That is, it is made up of legends invented in historical times to give the cause of existing facts or customs. The story of the rape of the Sabine women is an example. In historical times the Romans were curious to find an explanation for a certain part of the marriage ceremony (*confarreatio*) which they had inherited from their ancestors. There were other forms of the marriage ceremony common among them at this time, but in this, which was the oldest, and savored of antiquity, the groom tore the bride from the arms of her family as though by force. What was the origin of this custom? they asked. In answer to this some suggested one reason and others another. Finally, the tale was invented that, when Romulus was king, there were but few women at Rome, and that, to supply themselves with wives, his subjects stole the wives and daughters of their neighbors. Now, in point of fact, it surely was not in memory of this that the show of violence was employed in the *confarreatio*. If there is any explanation to be found for it, it will not be in any incident of

Roman history. This would be utterly unsatisfactory, because this form of ceremony is the property, not of the Romans alone, but of many primitive peoples. When once advanced, however, the story, because it seemed plausible, was repeated by many, at first only as probable, but in the end it took on the dignity of history, and as such has come down to us.

**6. The Teachings of Euhemerus.** — Another large section of these legends is taken to owe its origin to the influence of what is known as *euhemerism*. Euhemerus was a Sicilian Greek, who wrote a book about the nature of the gods. He taught that the gods were only men, deified by the imagination of their worshipers, and that all the stories current about their exploits in heaven were in reality the records of men's deeds on earth, transferred by superstition to the upper world. Jupiter, for instance, he said, had in point of fact been a king in Crete, and during his life as a man he had done the things which were told and believed about him as a god. This crude form of skepticism had, of course, suggested itself to the minds of a good many people before Euhemerus put it in literary shape, and it takes its name from him only because he was so able an advocate of it. A like way of thinking had been popular at Rome, from how early time we do not know. Men groping in the dark, without any explanation available to tell them the source of the myths they were taught to believe, naturally noticed the resemblance between the achievements of their gods and those which would be performed by men, and came in the end to ask, Were they not really human like ourselves, and are we not mistaken in regarding them as anything else? There has been some tendency, in modern times, to regard myths in this style, as a kind of distorted history, but it has not met with any great favor. In Rome, however, the effect of the notion was to humanize permanently many common tales which had been told of the gods and really belonged to mythology, and to introduce them into history as the exploits of men. Thus, for instance, it is guessed that some parts of the Romulus-and-Remus story may have come into existence. At first, they were twin gods, the Lares of the city. Then they were debased in the general view into men, and as such were regarded as the founders of the state.

7. **The Contribution of Deliberate Invention.**—Finally, a great many of these legends seem to have been deliberate inventions, made at a later time, by Greeks or others, who were familiar with the stories of Greek history. It is easy to see instances of this where they really do not exist. A vein of similar myth runs through the legendary period of most nations' records, and it is only a very superficial sort of criticism which regards this as an evidence that they have borrowed from one another. But, on the other hand, we can give one or two examples which are illustrative and also quite beyond question. Take the story of the capture of Gabii by the Romans under Tarquinius Superbus. It says that when the king sought to reduce the city of Gabii by force of arms, he could not, and

so had to resort to stratagem. His son Sextus, covered with wounds and gore, went to the town, as though fleeing from the Romans, and induced the Gabians to give him protection and shelter. When he had established himself in their confidence, he secretly sent a messenger to his father, asking for instructions as to how he should proceed in order to take the city. Tarquinius sent no answer in words, but, walking through his garden, struck off with a stick the tallest poppies which were growing there. When the messenger reported this to Sextus, he understood its meaning, and, by bringing false accusations against the chief men of Gabii, had them put to death. Finally, when the city was weakened by their loss, he surrendered it to the king. Such a story is clearly neither impossible nor involved in destructive obscurities and contradictions. Further than this, it is of a texture so simple that it might have been preserved for a hundred years or more without the help of written records. It is, in this way, quite impregnable against assault from any of these quarters. There is nothing to suggest that it was invented to explain any existing fact or custom, and it belongs to a period much later than that with reference to which the theory of Euhemerus was applied. If, however, we turn to the pages of the Greek writer Herodotus, we shall find, in spite of all this, that the only things that have to do with Roman history in the story are the names of the characters. The stratagem of Sextus and his father is there told in full detail with regard to Cyrus the Great and his capture of Babylon, while the incident of the poppy-heads belongs to the life of Periander, the tyrant of Corinth. In the Roman legend these two entirely unrelated anecdotes were somehow fastened together. In this form they were deliberately transplanted with slight variations from their original connection, and incorporated by repetition in Roman history, where we find them.

8. **Can we know anything, then, about Early Roman History?**—If the material thus accumulated have any value, it suggests how futile it is to try to thread one's way through the mazes of the city's early history with no other guidance than that afforded by the ancient writers. Under the most and least favorable view alike, they can secure for us something, but at any rate for the period prior to the third century it is only the merest framework. Oral tradition alone is competent proof for the fact that there were once kings at Rome, but if we seek for details it must be from other sources. Now, it is nothing better than a prejudice which estimates the testimony of words, spoken or written, as the highest and most trustworthy kind of evidence. Men's recollections of what they have seen and done are quickly dimmed by time, and even in so far as they are retained, are distorted or colored by the medium through which they view them. The same scenes present a hundred different aspects to a hundred different observers, because their education or their instincts lead them to attach unequal importance to the points in which they feel interest. And, again, how many can present to

another with any accuracy the picture which they see clearly themselves? Will not diffidence or too much zeal, carelessness or incapacity, suggest the use of words which make the meaning very remote from the one it was intended to convey? The evidence of eye-witnesses, therefore, is in any case only one sort among many which the careful seeker after truth relies on, and while its loss is a serious disadvantage, it never leaves him without resources. If one, for example, could know at about what time the *Cloaca Maxima* ("the big sewer") was built at Rome, he could get, in this way, as valuable information concerning contemporary civilization as a volume of descriptive essays would give him. Now, are there any such sources of knowledge for the period under discussion, and can we learn anything from them? To this it may be answered that there are some, but that they tell us nothing about men and battles. There have been many attempts in recent years to construct anew the history of the kings, winnowing the true from the false, but, in spite of their cleverness and their interest, they have been quite abortive. We can never hope to know of early Rome in the same personal way as we do of a modern nation. But about the city's life and the growth of its institutions we can get a good deal from one quarter and another to supplement and correct that given us by the ancients. With the help of this we can learn no little concerning very important things of even the earliest times.

9. **How the Science of Language helps**

us. — Modern research, which has developed the science of language, has supplied us with some testimony which is very valuable for some purposes, and worth at least something for others. We can not here explain how it teaches us about the prehistoric relations of the Romans to the other members of the Indo-European family, which belongs rather to the department of language than to that of history, but we can take an example or two of its suggestiveness in matters of a somewhat later time. If, for instance, we should discover in the Samnites' country tablets of stone inscribed with words in the Samnite tongue, and, on examination, we should find that these bore a very close resemblance in root and method of inflection to Latin words, we might infer that the Samnites and the Latins were of the same race. This, to be sure, would be by no means certain, because language is not always an indication of race. We ourselves see proofs of this every day, and in history we easily remember that the conquering Normans took the tongue of the English, and the conquered Gauls that of the Romans. But, nevertheless, we should get here at least a hint, to be confirmed or rejected by the contributions of other sources. Another example, however, will show that such evidence, even in its unsupported shape, will sometimes be very convincing. If one were writing a history of Roman commerce, he would search in vain through Livy and Dionysius for information about its direction in early times. Did the early Romans trade with the Greeks or with the Spaniards, with the Gauls or with the

Egyptians? There are a good many things, of course, which would assist in framing an answer to this question, but no one of them is more valuable than what is suggested by the presence, in the Latin language and in the Greek of Sicily and Campania, of many words, mutually borrowed, which signify the commodities and instruments of commerce. If the Romans incorporated in their language the forms of Greek words, which were employed in the Doric section of Magna Græcia, and borrowed nothing from the Achæan cities; and if, at the same time, the Achæan dialects bear no traces of contact with the Latin, while the Sicilian Greek had many terms such as the Romans used for the purposes of trade, we have here testimony of the highest order for the subject under consideration. This will prove, perhaps better than anything else could, that the Romans knew the Dorian Greeks who lived in Italy and met them in commerce, at this early time, at least more closely than they did the other races which surrounded them.

10. **Etymological Evidence.**—Or let us take a single word, and see what its etymology teaches about social usages with which, at first glance, it has no connection. In the view of Roman law, property was divisible into *res mancipi* and *res nec mancipi*, or into things the sale of which had to be accompanied by a certain prescribed ceremony in order to insure its validity, and those which passed freely without any such ceremony. In historical times, even if the owner agreed to sell and the purchaser paid the price demanded, such things as

land, buildings, slaves, horses, and cattle could not be acquired unless the sale was made in the presence of five witnesses, and with the minute observance of a series of formalities which we need not describe, but which were included in late Latin under the name *mancipatio*. The reason why the transfer of these was fenced in in this way, while the ordinary commodities of every-day life were bought and sold as they are with us, was that, at the time when this custom came into existence, such things were esteemed more highly in the popular view. In the same manner, in English law, land which got undue importance as a species of property from the feudal system, could not be disposed of without a great deal more ceremony than was required in the case of personalty. The name *mancipium*, or *mancipatio* (*manus*, " the hand," and *capio*, " to take,"), applied to the transaction, proves that its most characteristic feature was displayed when the buyer grasped with his hand, before the witnesses, the property, which thus became his. Such a performance was very appropriate to give publicity to the sale of a slave or a horse or a cow, but it clearly had no reference, at the beginning, to land, for this, of course, could not be the subject of manual delivery. The inference, then, is that land and buildings were not originally *res mancipi*, and that the ceremony with which they afterward were transferred was, in the first instance, employed only in the case of the other things included under this name. Now, it is quite impossible that the sale of land and buildings was ever a matter of less formality than that of the other *res mancipi*, and that restrictions grew up around it in the course of time. The whole history of Roman law forbids this theory, because it is a history of the removal of formalities, not of their imposition. And, in any event, land and buildings must always have stood as high in popular esteem as slaves and cattle. On the contrary, what all this means is that land and buildings were once not bought and sold at all at Rome, and that, when they began to be, they were classed along with these other things, whose importance was indicated by the formalities which accompanied their alienation. The etymology of a single word, in this way, informs us that there was a time when the Romans held their real estate in common, or when, if they held it in severalty, they had no right to part with this ownership.

11. **The Contribution of Comparative Law.**—We learn this fact, however, from still another source which is available, in general, for information about nations which had attained to considerable civilization before their history began. The study of the political and social institutions of a great many people has made it quite clear that they all tend to pass through the same stages of development from the simplest barbarism up to the high complexity of civilization. This belief has been arrived at after the examination of the life of many barbarous tribes, of the remains of ancient empires, and of the customs, both living and obsolete, of the nations of to-day. The science is still in its infancy, and has thus far been concerned chiefly

with the accumulation of facts which have yet to be arranged and compared. The results of this work promise to be of the utmost value. We have in the case of no people complete records from the beginning, and even those which run back to the most remote period present gaps where we should, perhaps, least of all be willing to have them. But according to this view, if we spread out in tabular form the steps in the growth of all the nations in the world of which we have any knowledge, and place them side by side, we can supply from one that which may be lacking in another. We shall show, in another connection, that, when Roman history begins, individuals did own real estate in the city, but under certain restrictions, which hinted that this had not always been so. Now, we know something about some countries, where all the land belongs to the community and the individual owns his share of the products of the soil only, and not the soil itself. There are others where a transition is making from this system to such a one as is common nowadays. The restrictions which attended land-holding at Rome at the dawn of history bear traces of both of these sorts of tenure— of the first in some degree, and of the second very conspicuously. We thus have a gleam of light from an earlier time to direct our investigations, and we can borrow from the records of other nations the preliminary stages which we can not find in its own, and construct with accuracy a history of land-holding at Rome from the earliest to the latest date. Civilizations as remote from each other as those of

England and Java, of Germany and Russia and India, contribute to this object. These all present the phenomenon of a primitive communal ownership of land, ending or tending to end in approximately the same form which was in vogue at Rome when we first hear anything about her. The inference is, therefore, if we treat the nations of the world as a whole, that here, too, this system had just reached its conclusion.

12. **Inferences from the Later History of the City.**—Finally, the institutions of the city in a later time, when we have tolerably complete information about them, present many facts which are suggestive of their previous history. Obsolete customs, and officials endowed with great nominal powers but no real ones, pointed to a time when the customs had a meaning and the magistracy's functions were not formalities, but essential to the state's political machinery. We can learn in this way, for example, about the sphere and the duties of the king. There were no kings at Rome in historical times, but there were the so-called curule magistrates who filled the king's place. Their powers were not in detail the same as his, because, of course, the growth of the city had given birth to new avenues for governmental activity, but in a broad way there was a correspondence. The king's *imperium*, we know from a trustworthy tradition, was bestowed on him by a law enacted in the *comitia curiata*, the people's primitive legislative assembly. The *comitia curiata*, as we shall presently see, continued to meet in historical times, in a purely formal way, to con-

fer the *imperium* on such officers as were entitled to it. The law which they passed for this purpose was a necessary preliminary, even under the republic, to commanding the army or exercising judicial functions of any kind. So we infer that it conferred similar powers on the king, who thus is proved to have been general and judge. Or, again, as the presiding officials in the popular assemblies of the republic alone of those present there could speak in support of a measure or against it, we infer that the king alone harangued the people at their meetings in regal times, because the course of the constitution's development had been to diminish the magistrates' influence, not to heighten it. Not to pursue this so far as to anticipate the pages which will follow, if we keep in view this possibility of constructing the past and unknown from that which is later and historical, we shall constantly see places in the city's record, as it is disclosed, which throw light on the obscurities covering the beginning.

13. **What we can learn from these Sources.**—When we find fair inferences from several such sorts of evidence as these, agreeing to confirm a view which has been taken about any point in Roman history, we are quite justified in considering it established. When light is thrown upon it from only one source, it will be at the best uncertain and a matter of opinion. The opinions of those, however, whose good judgment has been shown from their treatment of places where the evidence is more full, are worthy of the most con-

sideration here also, and may be taken as final. But, after all has been collected which the mute testimony of things and the authority of modern scholars afford, the human side of early Roman history is still for the most part hidden from us. This is unfortunate, because it is both entertaining and profitable to study about great men and their motives, and to read in detail the annals of the common people's simple lives. But our regret on this account may be tempered here by the thought that the sources of information which we have are especially valuable for those very things for which Roman history ought most of all to be studied. When we follow the career of the Hebrews, in the Bible, it is, of course, important to stop over their wars and to understand their system of government, but the great thing is to learn about their ideas on religion, and to see how these were developed. For, while their success in war was not particularly noteworthy, and their political system was quite rudimentary and did not count for much in the world, their conception of God's nature was so high that it has survived through the ages, and gladdens and directs our lives to-day. In the same manner, it would make very little difference to us if we knew nothing about Nikias the Greek and the siege of Syracuse, or about Lysander and the battle of Ægospotami. But it is quite essential, if we are to be educated men and get the joys which come from the things of the mind, that we should have some acquaintance with what Homer and Æschylus and Plato wrote, and with the frieze which Phidias made for the Parthenon. And this is because Greek literature and Greek art are immortal, and the principles to which they give expression are the ones by which we must be guided in order either to appreciate or produce what is beautiful. Rome's claim to consideration is from an entirely different stand-point. Roman literature, for instance, is not exceptionally interesting, or original, or pleasing; and some critics have gone so far as to say that nothing has been written in Latin which has not been better written in some other language. But, in matters of statecraft and jurisprudence, the modern world owes a great debt to ancient Rome. She worked out to success or failure most of the problems which present themselves to the practical statesman and law-maker of these days. Her ideas, therefore, on such things ought especially to be looked for in the study of her history, and these, more readily, perhaps, than anything else, can be learned from the sources of information which we have.

## CHAPTER II.

### THE STRUCTURE OF ANCIENT SOCIETY.

1. **The Roman Family.**—When we begin to study Roman history, no matter what the period, we are soon confronted by an institution which is quite foreign to anything existing at the present day. This is the *patria potestas*, or the peculiar power which a Roman father had over the members of his family. In the last years of the empire traces of it are still to be found, and at the outset it is the most conspicuous feature of the city's social system. A man's family, in this sense, consisted of all his descendants to the remotest generations, provided their relationship with him could be traced through males. Marriage was a religious ceremony (*confarreatio*), and, when his sons took wives, they brought them by means of it under his control. All their children, then, to the farthest limit, were also included in the same body. His daughters, on the other hand, became free as to him by their marriage, because they passed into the membership of another family. The relatives they thus acquired, and their own children, were counted as no kin of their father's family, because, in general, there was no such thing as relationship through women. Persons thus

connected were called cognates (*cognati*), and between them early Roman law recognized no tie of blood. Those who were related through males were called agnates (*agnati*), and over this agnatic family the father (*pater familias*) exercised unlimited sway. All its members were to him as his slaves or his property, and under a bondage which was life-long and quite complete. He could sell or kill them, and all which they had was his. There was no tribunal before which he had to account for his use of this authority, for within the limits of the family he was king and priest. As king, he administered justice, apportioned burdens, and distributed rewards. As priest, he offered sacrifices on the family's behalf at the family's altar to the family's gods. Having learned all this, if we knew nothing more about the structure of Roman society, we should say at any rate that it differed from modern society in that the unit was not the individual, as it is in our day, but this agnatic family.

2. **The Beginnings of Rome.**—In point of fact, however, the *patria potestas* and what followed from it were of the widest significance in giving shape and color to the city's political as well as to its social institutions. We shall get some proof of this if we consider the nature of Rome's primary political organism, the clan (*gens*, *cf.* root *gen*, seen in *gigno*). When Roman history begins, there were within the city, and subordinate to the common city government, a large number of smaller bodies, each of which preserved its individuality and some semblance of governmental machinery. These were

clans, and in prehistoric times each of them is taken to have had an independent political existence, living apart, worshiping its own gods, and ruled over by its own chieftain. This clan organization is not supposed to have been peculiar at all to Rome, but ancient society in general was composed of an indefinite number of such bodies, which, at the outset, treated with each other in a small way as nations might treat with each other to-day. It needs to be noted, however, that, at any rate, so far as Rome is concerned, this is a matter of inference, not of historical proof. The earliest political divisions in Latium, of which we have any trace, consisted of such clans united into communities. If they ever existed separately, therefore, their union must have been deliberate and artificial, and the body thus formed was the canton (*civitas*, or *populus*). Each canton had a fixed common stronghold (*capitolium*, "height," or *arx* (*cf. arceo*), "citadel,") situated on some central elevation. The clans dwelt around in hamlets (*vici*, or *pagi*) scattered through the canton. Originally, the central stronghold was not a place of residence like the *pagi*, but a place of refuge, whither the allied clans might retreat in case of danger from invasion, and a place of meeting, where they assembled for a common religious worship, for the holding of festivals and markets, and for the adjustment of disputes. Most of the cities in the plain of Latium, of which we hear in Roman history, were, in their origin, simply the sites of canton-centers of this character. The earliest of them to be founded were on the Alban hills, whose lofty position rendered them easy of fortification. Such, too, was the beginning of towns like Lanuvium, Aricia, and Tusculum. Where the Apennines extend out into the Campagna, towns like Tibur and Præneste grew up. On elevations near the coast were Laurentum and Lavinium, and, near the mouth of the Tiber, Rome herself came to be a city, in the first place, because she was adapted to be a place of refuge for the clans about her.

3. **What was a Clan?**—In all of this, therefore, the clan seems to lie at the very foundation, and ought to be defined. We shall call it a widened family. This is only one of several possible definitions, and in giving it here we do not vouch at all for its historical correctness. Assuming it for the present, however, to be accurate, all the members of a clan were related by blood. Any clan in the beginning, of course, must have been simply a family. When it grew so large as to be divided into sections, the sections were known as families (*familiæ*), and their union was the clan. In this view, the family, as we find it existing in the Roman state, was a subdivision of the clan. In other words, historically, families did not unite to form clans, but the clan was the primitive thing, and the families were its branches. Men thus recognized kinship of a double character. They were related to all the members of their clan as *gentiles*, and again more closely to all the members of their branch of the clan at once as *gentiles* and also as *agnati*. As already stated, men belonged to the same family (*agnati*) when they could trace their descent through males

from a common ancestor who gave its name to the family, or, what is the same thing, was its *eponym*. Between the members of a clan the chief evidence of relationship in historical times was tradition. They found themselves bearing a common name and having a common religious worship. They believed that they were descended from a common ancestor, but, as the organization had existed from before the dawn of history, it was not possible for them to know anything certain as to how they were connected with their *eponym*. The primitive social group, then, was in this way made up of kinsmen, governed in the same way and by the same authority as the family. From this up to the highest social group of ancient society there was an orderly development, shaped and colored by this beginning, families of kinsmen forming clans of kinsmen, and clans of kinsmen, as time grew old, uniting artificially to make the state.

4. **The Patriarchal Theory.**—We have thus outlined what is known as the patriarchal theory of society, and hinted at its application to certain facts in Roman history. It should be remembered, however, that it is only a theory, and that it is open to some apparent and to some real criticism. As stated in the categorical way in which we have given it, it is assailable from several sides. It is not possible, of course, nor desirable to consider all of its weaknesses here, but something needs to be said of them in order to show both its meaning and its limits. One, and perhaps the least serious, objection is that it has an exact and artificial form

which makes it appear untenable of men living in society. Such rigid exclusions and inclusions would be possible with puppets moved hither and thither by a master-mind, but, where men are the factors, we expect more latitude and greater flexibility. The definiteness of growth from family into clan, and then back from clan to families with all the subsequent unions up to the latest, seems very unreasonable. This, however, is more a fault of recital than of fact. It should be borne in mind that in the statement of all social phenomena it is necessary to follow a simple line of essentials, and that the imagination of the student has to be employed to blur the outlines. For example, what is here given is of a typical family and clan, to which it is not claimed that any actual family or clan ever corresponded in full detail. Under this theory strangers were admitted, in fact, into families by various forms of adoption, and families incorporated into clans with which they had no tie of blood. Consanguineous clans also were from time to time disrupted from one cause or another; and, again, clans of an entirely artificial character, whose members came from anywhere, and bore no relationship to each other, were constantly formed under all sorts of incentives. According to the theory, however, the primitive thing was the clan of kinsmen divided into families of kinsmen, and through all, this remained the type after which the others were modeled by analogy.

5. **The Patriarchal Theory** (*continued*).— But there are other weaknesses which are more real. For one thing, the source of its fundamental idea,

the *patria potestas*, is a mystery. If you ask an advocate of the patriarchal theory how it was that the father had such extraordinary and undisputed authority in primitive society, he will answer that it is impossible to tell. But a system whose basis is a mystery must rest on strong historical evidence, or else confess that there are other systems back of it, out of which it may have been developed. Here, again, are two other heads under which very just criticism can be made on the theory. It claims to be historical in its methods, and yet to tell about the beginnings of things. But history can not tell us about the beginnings of things, for things began long before any of the sources of history existed. But, if this simply means that the patriarchal form of government is the earliest of known forms, then this conclusion ought to be based on evidence collected from every quarter. In point of fact, however, sole reliance for proof has been put on a few Indo-European and Semitic races in a comparatively advanced stage of civilization. The vast mass of facts, which might be contributed by the rest of the world, has not been drawn on. But, when these have been collated, they present difficulty after difficulty, which the patriarchal theory does not meet; and yet it must meet them if the theory is to stand in the form in which it has been advanced.

**6. The Application of these Criticisms to Roman History.**—The weight of these objections is so very serious as to have given rise to an entirely different course of speculation. This denies that the family form of society was primitive, and that the clan was based on kinship. It holds that society began as a promiscuous horde, in which marriage was not recognized, and that, when it emerged from this, it was in the form of a tribe. Clans were, in this view, subdivisions of the tribe, made on some principle not very clear. As a theory of social development, all this is as yet quite unformed, but for purposes of destructive criticism it has great value. Because of it we are not justified in labeling any of the known social organisms as primitive to the exclusion of the others, nor can we hold it proved that the original clan was in fact consanguineous. But this is not necessary for the purposes of Roman constitutional history. It is enough that the members of a Roman clan always thought of themselves as thus related, and that this belief was always with them strong enough to shape their actions. Its historical truth is a matter of no moment. The influence of their belief on the development of their institutions was as great as the influence of the fact would have been. In this sense, and with these limitations, it may be granted that the patriarchal theory was true of the Romans. This brings us back again to the statement of Rome's origin as a canton-center in the plain of Latium.

7. **The Early Roman Religion.** — In order to understand the social and political life of the men who lived in this community, we have to know something about their notions on several other matters. It is important, as we shall see, to know

that they believed in the existence of spirits, and that they made some of them the objects of worship. This belief seems to be shared by all people in the primitive stages of civilization. That is, all known religions, in spite of their great and many differences, have this conception in common. It must, therefore, belong to a very early stage in their development, because we find it the property of races which are very low in the intellectual scale. The Greeks and the Romans thus, before they parted from each other in prehistoric times, believed that the world was peopled by beings other than those which we can see or feel. These beings in this primitive view appear not to have been abstractions, but to have been the doubles of things which could be seen or felt. Physical things, whether living or lifeless, had ghostly counterparts which dwelt in them or about them. Thus there would be a spirit corresponding to the sky which one could see, and another corresponding to the person of the man with whom one talked and lived. These ghostly counterparts were at first always thought of in connection with the things to which they belonged. Before the beginning of Rome's separate history, however, some of them had been divorced from the objects to which they had originally been attached, and personified or anthropomorphized. This was the case with the spirits of some of the more conspicuous objects of nature, like the firmament, the spirit of which was thus made into the god *Jupiter* of the Romans, or *Zeus pater* of the Greeks. In the same way the spirit corresponding to the hearth-fire became the goddess *Vesta* of the Romans and *Hestia* of the Greeks. This separation and personification of the spirits, however, had not been carried very far at this date, as the small number of cognate words found in the two languages among the names of divinities shows.

8. **The Early Roman Religion** (*continued*).— Now, the Roman religion itself from the time of its independent existence continued to develop along these two lines. On the one hand, it carried out this idea of the existence of ghosts or doubles with a completeness and consistency which never flinched. On the other, the spirits of specific objects were every now and then detached from their special connection and entered into the body of general deities. But it is with the first of these methods of god-making alone that we are at present concerned, because the significance of the second belongs to a later period of the city's history. In the primitive Roman conception, then, every thing, every place, every act, every thought, had a spiritual counterpart which ruled and directed it, but which in respect to other objects was quite powerless. The world of ghosts or doubles was as populous as the real world was full of things which could be seen or conceived. Nobody could say how many divinities of this sort there were, because their number was of course limitless. For example, sixty or more gods are enumerated which had to do with the growth of the human body, like "*Vagitanus*, who opened the mouth of the infant for his first cry;

*Cunina*, who guarded the cradle; *Educa*, who taught the infant to eat; *Potina*, who taught him to drink; *Ossipago*, who knit the bones. For husbandry there were gods like *Nodutus*, who caused the joints of the stalks to grow; *Volutina*, who wrapped them in their leaf-sheaths; *Patelina*, who opened the wrappings that the ear might come out in due season; *Hostilina*, who made the crop even in its ears; down to *Runcina*, who presided over the pulling of the roots from the ground." Deities of this nature, bearing names the etymology of which was so obvious, were of course strictly limited in their sphere of action. No one would think of calling on the divinity *Terminus* ("the boundary") for help in the acquisition of wealth, or of thanking the god *Febris* ("fever") because he had survived the dangers of a sea-voyage. For each such thing its appropriate spirit either already existed, or was invented as the need arose. When Hannibal, for instance, marching on the city, repented of his purpose and turned away, the Romans built a temple in honor of *Deus Rediculus* ("the god who had caused the departure"). Or, again, when, about 250 B. C., silver was introduced into the Roman coinage, *Æsculanus*, the ancient spirit of copper money, was at once taken to have begotten a son, *Argentinus*. It all seems like a sort of ghostly mockery of mortal things — as though shadows danced in imitation of all that men could think or do.

**9. The Early Romans' Ideas about the Dead.**—The mental attitude, thus described, is certainly very remarkable, and immediately invites inquiry as to its origin. If there is any explanation forthcoming, it will have to be one which will account also for their notions about the doubles, or *genii*, of men. These were fully as strange as their other conceptions which we have discussed, and are clearly parts of the same way of thinking. They believed that the souls of men did not die with their bodies, but that they survived after the death of the men to whom they were attached. They did not conceive of them, in the beginning, as inhabiting in a company some common spirit-land, but as hovering in isolation about the tomb where the lifeless body was interred. If the body were not interred, neither would the soul have a resting-place, but would wander as an evil spirit over the earth—unhappy, and making others so. Moreover, burial of the body was not in itself sufficient, but it needed, in addition, care and attention from the living. This care and attention were to be shown by giving to it, near the tomb at regular intervals, offerings of food and of drink. These it was thought of at first as requiring after death as much as it had required them when living. If it was honored in this simple way, its soul or *genius* became a propitious deity, and assisted those who cared for it. If for any reason, however, these offerings were ever interrupted, the soul at once became as that of the unburied—unhappy, and making others so. Men, therefore, sought to leave behind them, when their life ended, those who would continue these gifts of food and drink, which were to insure their eternal happiness. And in like manner, as long as they lived, they sacrificed to their ancestors who were dead, and prayed them to be kind, and aid them with their ghostly power in return for this service.

10. **The Influence of these Beliefs within the Family.**—This custom of worshiping the dead ancestors has been advanced by some as an explanation of the origin of the *patria potestas*. The selection of the dead father, however, in this way, as the object of particular worship, would seem to be the result of his power when alive rather than the cause of it. But, when once established in the popular mind as true, this religious incentive must have co-operated powerfully with every other motive in maintaining the peculiar form of the Roman family. All a man's descendants were thus linked together, not, as they are in modern times, by a feeble chain of instinctive affection, but as a close corporation for a religious purpose of the utmost importance. The father's control, whatever its origin, was re-enforced by his sacred character as chief priest to offer sacrifices with the co-operation of his children. In the same way additional sanction was given to the system of reckoning relationship through males only. Marriage was a religious ceremony, because it admitted a stranger into participation in the family sacrifices. Henceforth the wife's duty was at the altar of her husband. Those, therefore, who were born from her had no heritable connection with her father's family, because they could not be called on to perform the sac-

rifices to its dead, nor did they share in their ghostly favor. The family property, the fund out of which the offerings were made, could not pass to them any more than to any other strangers. Kinship was, then, based on a religious motive, and its evidence was not blood but a common worship.

11. **The Influence of these Beliefs without the Family.**—Now, the clan, the primary political organism in the view we have elaborated, has been defined as a widened family, and, like the narrower family, acknowledged common ancestors to whom all the clansmen paid sacrifices of the same character as those offered in each household. This custom stands quite independent of the opinion which may be held about the clan's nature. If the clan really grew out of a family, and again in turn divided into families, the ancestors worshiped had an historical claim to veneration from the clansmen. If, on the other hand, the clan was an artificial subdivision of some pre-existing larger body, as is held by some, or, if it was an artificial union of families which really had no relationship with each other, then both this belief in the existence of common ancestors and their worship had a purely fictitious basis. When the canton was formed by the union of clans, the incentive, of course, was contiguity of territory. Clans united because they lived near each other. But the clansmen did not acknowledge this. They feigned, on the contrary, that they were brought together by ties of kin, and thought of the canton as having common ancestors to whom wor-

ship was to be paid after the form employed by the clan and the family. This extension of a law or custom by analogy, to cover ground to which it strictly does not apply at all, is called a "legal fiction." The use of this device was a powerful force in molding ancient law and political institutions, not only at Rome but also among all early people. The method of its alleged operation in this particular case is quite clear, and will serve as a general illustration. When men met as a family they found that, by a custom, the origin of which none of them had seen, they first of all recognized by religious observances the claims of their dead ancestors. This was also the case when they assembled as members of a clan. When the canton was formed artificially, no such ceremonies, as a matter of course, marked its gatherings. But the exception was felt to be strange and irksome, and was deliberately removed. Then sacrifices were offered to feigned canton ancestors, who, as time passed by, came to be viewed as though they were real and historical.

12. **The City of Rome.**—If these theories have any value, this fictional extension had to be carried in the case of Rome still one stage further, because the city grew out of the union of three cantons or clan-communities. One of these was composed of the clans of the Ramnes, a Latin people who dwelt on the slopes and at the base of the Palatine Hill, and whose stronghold was on its summit. Their territory formed the first city, the "square Rome" (*Roma quadrata*). Over against

them, on the Quirinal, lived the Tities, who seem perhaps to have been Sabines. These cantons uniting made Rome. Afterward the Luceres, apparently of Latin race, but whose previous history is all unknown to us, were admitted. When the three were consolidated in this way, they formed a new canton, of which each of the old ones became a tribe (*tribus*). Together they occupied at the outset a narrow strip of land on both sides of the Tiber as far as its mouth, but inland their territory was limited in any direction at a distance of five miles by the territory of adjacent canton-centers.

## CHAPTER III.

### ROME UNDER THE KINGS.

1. **The Power of the King.**—In prehistoric times, when clans united into cantons, the government of the canton naturally came to be modeled after that of its component clans. When several cantons united again as tribes to make a new canton, as was the case at Rome, the form of the primitive clan government was still followed. As we have already seen, the clan as well as the family had a natural head, who ruled over it with absolute power and offered sacrifices on its behalf to the gods. The natural head of the family was, of course, the father. The natural head of the clan was the oldest male descendant in the oldest line from the clan's *eponym*. But when the canton was formed out of clans which united without any real blood relationship, simply because they lived near one another, it became necessary to choose a leader for it, because nature had provided none. To this position any able-bodied freeman in the community was eligible, and in the beginning every freeman had a voice in the choice of its occupant. When the leader (*rex* or *dictator*) had been selected, he at once, by universal consent, came to stand to the

state in precisely the same relation as the father did to the family. This was a legal fiction of a piece with that which made all the members of a clan kinsmen. The Romans at this early time were not able to conceive of a government constructed on any other plan than this, which they knew so well because they had always used it in the family and the clan. The king, therefore, was the state's high-priest, and, to perfect the parallel, he was assisted in the sacred duties of this office by six vestal virgins, who kept the fire burning in the *atrium* of the state, as the mother and daughters did in the *atrium* of the household. In the second place, his kingly power (*imperium*) was, like the *patria potestas*, absolute over his subjects. He could at his will deprive a citizen of his life or his liberty, as the father could, a child. He was the sole judge in all civil and criminal disputes, and from his decision there was no appeal. The public treasury was under his control, and, when there was a war, he called out and commanded the army, and divided the booty in case of victory among the warriors according to his own caprice. Like the father in the family, he held his *imperium* as long as he lived. When the father died, the next of kin succeeded him. The king, before his death, nominated his successor, who was to take his place at the head of the state if his nomination were confirmed by the freemen of the community.

2. **Restrictions on the King's Power.**—So great power put into the hands of one man is quite contrary to anything which exists nowadays in civ-

ilized nations. The most despotic of governments falls far short of this extreme. But we must remember that, when this constitution came into being, Rome was not a nation, but a city of small size, where every freeman might know and be known by the king. Again, it was easy for the Romans to submit to authority, because they had all been under the *patria potestas* at some time during their lives, and many of them, in spite of years and honors, had not yet been emancipated from it. On the other hand, they knew that those who were called to the head of the state would have learned in advance how to use absolute power with self-restraint and discretion. This was because they would have been trained in its exercise as fathers and rulers in their own houses. In the family the father's control was limited by the sanctions of religion, which pronounced a father accursed who, for example, should sell his married son into slavery; by the fear of retaliation should he use his power to the uttermost; and by the customs of his ancestors (*mos majorum*), which determined the groove in which he must work. Now, all these things, and especially the *mos majorum*, operated as checks also on the caprice of the king. The king himself, in the beginning, was the source of law, but this beginning was before the formation of the city, when the community was nothing more than a clan. Primitive law was the arbitrary decision of a chieftain on a dispute which some of his subjects submitted to him. At first such decisions were irregular and unconnected, but in the end they acquired a certain uniformity, and those which were earlier shaped as precedents those which followed. These, together with such customs as grew up in other ways, had come, when the canton was formed, to have the binding force of law. The king's *imperium* allowed him to do anything which he pleased and dared, provided it was in execution of these customs of the ancestors. But there it stopped. When he proposed to alter them, he had first to obtain permission from the senate or council of elders, and from the whole people assembled for the purpose.

3. **The Comitia Curiata.**—In the beginning, any member of any one of the clans which were included in the three original Roman tribes, was a Roman citizen. So, too, were his children born in lawful wedlock, and those who were adopted by him according to the forms of law. Illegitimate children, on the other hand, were excluded from the number of citizens. These earliest Romans called themselves patricians (*patricii*, "children of their fathers"), for some reason about which we can not be sure. Perhaps it was in order to distinguish themselves from their illegitimate kinsmen and from such other people as lived about, having no pretense of blood connection with them, and who were, therefore, incapable of contracting lawful marriages according to the patricians' view of this religious ceremony. The patricians, as we have already seen, were grouped together in families, clans, and tribes, partly on the basis of blood relationship, but chiefly on the basis of common religious worship. Besides these groups, there was still another in the state,

the *curia*, or "ward," which stood between the clan and the tribe. In the earliest times, tradition said, ten families formed a clan, ten clans a *curia*, and ten *curiæ* a tribe. These numbers, if they ever had any historical existence, could not have maintained themselves for any length of time in the case of the clans and families, for such organisms of necessity would increase and decrease quite irregularly. About the nature of the *curia* we have practically no direct information. The organization had become a mere name at an early period in the city's history. Whether the members of a *curia* thought of themselves as having closer kinship with one another than with members of other *curiæ* is not clear. We know, however, that the *curiæ* were definite political subdivisions of the city, perhaps like modern wards, and that each *curia* had a common religious worship for its members' participation. Thus much, at any rate, is significant, because it has to do with the form of Rome's primitive popular assembly. When the king wanted to harangue the people (*populus, cf. populor*, "to devastate"), he called them to a *contio* (compounded of *co* and *venio*). But, if he wanted to propose to them action which implied a change in the organic law of the state, he summoned them to a *comitia* (compounded of *con* and *eo*). To this the name *comitia curiata* was given, because its members voted by *curiæ*. Each *curia* had one vote, the character of which was determined by a majority of its members, and a majority of the *curiæ* decided the matter for the *comitia*.

**4. The Functions of the Comitia Curiata.**
—When the freemen were thus assembled in response to his call, the king stated to them his proposals, and asked their indorsement. Here are some of the things for which their permission was necessary. No man could make a will, disposing of his property, without first consulting the people through the medium of the king. This was because, by the customs of the ancestors, property did not belong to the individual to bequeath at his caprice, but was his only as the representative of the family, to be transmitted on his death to the next of kin who should succeed him in maintaining the family sacrifices. The king could call out the troops for a defensive war on his own responsibility, but, for an offensive war, he had to obtain the permission of the people, because, in general, an offensive war implied a violation of a treaty with the city against which it was declared, and a treaty was, of course, a part of the law of the state. Again, pardon could not be given to a malefactor, once condemned, until all the citizens had expressed their opinion on the question in the *comitia*, for the sentence, when pronounced by the king, was like a statute, binding unless repealed by the regular course of procedure. And, for similar reasons, the admission of a stranger into a family, or of a new clan into a tribe, required the same formal consent if it were to be legal.

**5. The Senate and its Functions.**—In prehistoric times, the clans which subsequently united to form cantons had each possessed a monarchical constitution of its own. When the clan governments were merged in that of the canton, the monarchs (*reges*) of these clans became senators or elders in the new community. In the case of Rome the number of senators was three hundred, because in the beginning, as tradition said, there were three hundred clans. In regal times the king appointed the senators. Probably, at first, he chose one from each clan, honoring in this way some man whose age had given him experience and whose ability made his opinion entitled to consideration. Afterward, when the rigidity of the arrangement by clans was lost, the senators were selected from the whole body of the people, without any attempt at preserving the clan representation. Primarily the senate was not a legislative body. When the king died without having nominated his successor, the senators served successively as *interreges* ("kings for an interval"), for periods of five days each, until a *rex* was chosen. It was then their duty in turn, as they held the office, beginning with the second, to name to the *populus* a suitable man for king. The first *interrex* did not suggest a *rex*, because he had received his office, not by appointment but by lot. The second *interrex* and all who succeeded him, however, having been named each by his predecessor, had a clear title for the purpose. By this fiction the *rex* was always nominated by the monarch occupying the throne before him with an unbroken succession. This general duty was the first of the senate's original functions. Again, when the citizens had passed a law at the suggestion of the king, the senate had a right (*pa-*

*trum auctoritas*) to veto it, if it seemed contrary to the spirit of the city's institutions. Finally, as the senate was composed of men of experience and ability, the king used to consult it in times of personal doubt or national danger. When thus called on, the senators could offer advice to the king, who followed it or not according to his will.

6. **The Early Greatness of Rome.**—Rome's pre-eminence over her neighbors in primitive times seems to have been largely due to the advantages which her position gave her in a commercial direction. The immediate site of the city was surpassed in fertility and healthfulness by that of most of the Latin towns; and the Campagna, or plain about Rome, when compared, for example, with Campania, was not especially productive. But for commerce, as it was then carried on, her situation was well adapted. For one thing, the city was on the Tiber, fifteen miles from its mouth in a straight line, but twenty-seven if the windings of the river be followed. A close connection was thus made between it and the interior on the one hand and the coast on the other, and a highway formed for foreign and inland trade. Its remoteness from the sea saved it from the attacks of passing marauders, to which the Etruscan and Greek cities on the coast were exposed. At the same time, the shelter afforded by the river, which at Rome is twenty feet deep and three hundred feet wide, must have made it a well-known harbor on the unindented Italian coast. It was the natural market-place for the wide region drained by the Tiber and its tributa-

ries, because it was the place nearest to the sea which was capable of the fortification requisite for a city. Here the farmers from the Campagna brought their produce, and here the boatmen coming down the river stopped, as at the last point before they ventured on the sea, or to trade with the merchants from abroad. Long before the dawn of authentic history, the city had grown to be a compact and prosperous business center, inhabited by a trading and money-making people. These early Romans, however, were not an exclusively trading people, as for example were the inhabitants of some of the Etruscan towns, like Caere. They tilled the soil in their vicinity, and raised, as did their neighbors, grain and grapes, olives and figs, cattle and swine and poultry. With the Etruscans they exchanged cattle, slaves, and sometimes grain, for copper and silver, and with the copper and silver they bought from the Greeks of Magna Græcia and Sicily ornaments of gold, clay pottery, linen and leather, ivory and purple and frankincense. The people who lived in a community like this would naturally be of a strong and aggressive disposition. And such the early Romans were. Entering first as adventurers, attracted by the natural advantages of the situation, they formed a race whose character combined the alertness and intelligence of a commercial people with the stability and love of country which belong to a farming population.

7. **The Evidences of this Early Commercial Greatness.**—We state this view of Rome's

importance, as a commercial center in prehistoric times, without qualification, although it is by no means universally or even commonly acceded to. In the minds of many students of Roman history war and farming were, at the outset and for a long time, the only national occupations, and the early Romans were little better than savages, and their city, a collection of hovels. This opinion, it may be said in passing, is quite inconsistent with many traditions, generally accepted as trustworthy. Rome could not have been a village, but must have grown already before the dawn of authentic history into a large and wealthy city, if it be true, for example, that the public works, which are attributed to the kings, like the Capitoline Temple, the Circus Maximus, the wall of Servius, and the Cloaca Maxima, were really built by them, or if, in the original form of the *comitia centuriata*, the value of a man's vote varied with the amount of his property. But neither of these things is quite beyond dispute, and this whole subject, like everything about the period, must always be more or less a matter of uncertainty. Here, however, seems a good place to illustrate the sort of material out of which such a theory as we have advanced is constructed. There are available, then, several pieces of evidence which go to prove that Rome was a point of considerable trade from the earliest times. We give them one after the other: (1) The city's first colony was Ostia, a seaport town. This clearly was founded neither with a view to the military defenses of the city, nor because the country about it was good for farming, but to meet the purposes of commerce. Again (2), from time immemorial, duties were levied at Ostia on imports and exports intended for sale; and (3) strangers had been allowed the right of acquiring property at Rome with practically no restrictions. These, however, are not the devices and methods of farmers, but of men made shrewd and broad-minded by contact with the world. The presence of (4) the galley in the city's arms shows that trade on the sea was prominent in the life of the people; and, finally, as an argument from philology, we have (5) the interchange, between the Latin language and the Greek of Magna Græcia and Sicily, of many words for the commodities and instruments of commerce. Reference has already been made to this last as indicating the direction of early Roman trade, but, of course, it is equally valuable as establishing its existence. No one of these things by itself could shape our final judgment; and, even if we accept what they suggest when taken together, the inference will not be entirely free from doubt. We think, on the other hand, that their bearing is direct and quite conclusive.

8. **The Plebeians.**—We are now prepared to understand the origin of a distinct body of people which grew up alongside of the patricians of the Roman state during the latter part of the regal period and after its close. These were the plebeians (*plebs*, "the crowd," *cf. pleo*, to fill), who dwelt in the Roman territory both within and without the walls of the city. They did not belong to the old

clans which formed the three original tribes, nor did they have any real or pretended kinship with them, nor, for that matter, with one another, except within the ordinary limits of nature. They were, at the outset, simply an ill-assorted mass of residents, entirely outside of the orderly arrangement which we have described. There were three sources of this multitude:

I. When the city grew strong enough, it began to extend its boundaries, and first at the expense of the cantons nearest it, between the Tiber and the Anio. When Rome conquered a canton, she destroyed the walls of its citadel. Its inhabitants were sometimes permitted to occupy their villages as before, and sometimes were removed to Rome. In either case, Rome was henceforth to be their place of meeting and refuge, and they themselves, instead of being reduced to the condition of slaves, were attached to the state as non-citizens.

II. The relation of guest-friendship so called, in ancient times, could be entered into between individuals with their families and descendants, and also between individuals and a state or between two states. Provision for such guest-friendship was undoubtedly made in the treaties which bound together Rome on the one side and the various independent cities of its neighborhood on the other. Under these treaties citizens of one allied community were protected within the territory of another, and allowed to carry on trade there freely, and to hold real and personal property. The commercial advantages of Rome's situation attracted to it, in the course of time, a great many men from the Latin cities in the vicinity, who remained permanently settled there without acquiring Roman citizenship.

III. A third constituent element of the *plebs* was formed by the clients ("the listeners," *cluere*). It is very possible that, when the Romans came into Latium, they brought clients with them. These were non-freemen, either regarded as dependents of the whole clan or more commonly subject to the household jurisdiction of some *pater familias*, called, with reference to them, *patronus*. They differed widely from slaves in that they were allowed to hold property and engage in trade. New clients were in early times being constantly created in one of two ways: in the first place, foreigners coming to Rome might put themselves under the protection of some Roman citizen, to whom they thenceforth owed loyalty; in the second place, a slave, if freed, did not become a citizen, but a client of his former master's. The clients participated in a subordinate way in the religious worship of the clan and family, and were considered bound to stand by the members of their clan, sometimes with contributions from their property and sometimes with arms. In the beginning of the long struggle between the patricians and plebeians, the clients are represented as having sided with the former. But even then many of them must have appreciated the community of interests which united them with the other classes of plebeians; and afterward, when the lapse of time had weakened their sense of dependence on their patrons, they became, as a body, identified with the plebeians.

9. **The Primitive Political Condition of the Plebeians.**—The rights of a Roman citizen came, at a later period of the city's history, to be classified with great precision and many refinements, but here in the beginning, of course, were hazy and uncertain. One set of them, however, was clearly enough concerned with his capacity to participate in the affairs of the state, and another with his position before the law as a member of society. The first were his public rights, and the second his private rights. These last, under a subsequent legal arrangement, were all embraced under two heads: (1) the right of engaging in trade at Rome under the protection of the Roman laws concerning trade, which was called the *jus commerci*, and (2) the right of marrying a Roman citizen under the assurance that his children would be Roman citizens, and that he would have over them the control which the Roman constitution secured to fathers. This was called the *jus connubi*. All the plebeians seem to have enjoyed from the outset the *jus commerci*, which under the early kings can not have meant anything more than that they were protected in the acquisition of property equally with the patricians. When the regular Roman courts were invented, the first two classes of plebeians could use them freely, suing and maintaining their rights when sued, in their own names, but the clients had to bring their suits through the medium of their patrons. On the other hand, they

were all in general denied the *jus connubi*. Thus busy in trade, they rapidly gained property, and marrying among themselves and leaving their estates to their children, they came to rival the patricians in wealth and to excel them in numbers. All this while, however, they were rigidly excluded from participation in the government of the state. That is, no plebeian could be king, could sit in the senate, or vote in the *comitia curiata*. The reason for this was in no small degree religious, and of a piece with their exclusion from the *jus connubi*. The plebeian woman could not marry into a Roman family, because this would admit her to the worship of gods in whose favor she had no share. So the Romans resisted the admission of foreigners to political privileges, because they were not willing to intrust the sacrifices to the city's ancestors to men who had no kinship with them. This was a state of affairs which was long maintained, because there is nothing more powerful in its influence over men's minds than religious superstition, but in the end it had to yield to a more just and equal system.

# CHAPTER IV.

## THE EARLIEST REFORMS IN THE ROMAN CONSTITUTION.

1. **The Burdens of Citizenship.** — Under the original constitution of Rome, the patricians alone, as we have seen, enjoyed political rights in the state, but at the same time they were forced to bear the whole burden of political duties. In these last were included, for example, the tilling of the king's fields, the construction of public works and buildings, and the execution of the king's commands. In the earliest times there was little need of direct taxation, because the revenues from imports and exports, and the spoils of war, sufficed to meet the expenses of the state; but when for any reason the public treasury became empty, a *tributum*, or forced loan, was exacted from the patricians, to be paid back at some later time. Citizens alone, also, were liable to service in the army, and therefore on the patricians fell exclusively the dangers and toils of the city's wars. A state of affairs like this had the effect of making the plebeians a subject population, under the direct protection of the patricians. The political burdens, especially those connected with the army, grew heavier natu-

rally as the power of Rome increased, and it was seen to be an injustice that one part of the people, and that, too, the smaller part, should alone feel their weight. This led to the first important modification of the Roman constitution, which was made even before the close of the regal period. According to tradition, its author was the king Servius Tullius, and its general object was to make all men who held land in the state liable to military service. It thus conferred no political rights on the plebeians, but assigned to them their share of political duties.

2. **The Servian Classification.** — The arrangement which was made for this purpose has great significance, because in it another principle of classification than that which was based on the family was recognized for the first time. There is serious reason for doubting whether the details of the organization which have been given to us by the Latin and Greek writers refer to its original shape, and not rather to one which it assumed under some subsequent reform. But, however this may be, real or fictitious relationship seems not to have entered at all as a factor into the system. According to tradition, all the freeholders in the city between the ages of seventeen and sixty, with some exceptions, were divided, without distinction as to birth, into five classes (*classis*, " a summoning," *calo*) for service in the infantry according to the size of their estates. Those who were excepted served as horsemen. These were selected from among the very richest men in the state, some be-

cause they had served in the cavalry in the earlier arrangement of the army, and others on some other principle. The non-freeholders, too, were employed as workmen or musicians, or compelled to follow the army as a reserve, to be called on in an emergency, and orphans and widows were included by a tax placed on them for the cost and maintenance of the knights' horses. Of the five classes of infantry, the first contained the richest men, but the standard seems to have been placed low enough to make it the largest numerically. It and all the other classes were again divided into two sections, one containing all the men over forty-five years of age ; these were called "*seniores.*" The other contained all younger than that, and they were called "*juniores.*" At the first marshaling, the *seniores* in each class seem to have outnumbered the *juniores*. The members of the first class were required to come to the battle array in complete armor, while less was demanded of the other four. Each class was subdivided into centuries, or bodies of a hundred men each, for convenience in arranging the army. There were in all one hundred and ninety-three centuries, of which eighty were included in the first class, eighteen in the cavalry, five among the non-freeholders, and the rest in the other four classes. This absolute number and this apportionment were continued, as the population increased and the distribution of wealth altered, until the name century came to have a purely conventional meaning, even if it had any other in the beginning. Henceforth a careful census was taken every fourth year, and all freeholders were made subject to the *tributum*.

3. **How the Exercitus of Servius became the Comitia Centuriata.**—The arrangement of the people, thus described, was primarily made simply for military purposes. The primitive array of the army now gave place to a new order, and the Romans, plebeians as well as patricians, assembled at the call of the king in the Campus Martius in preparation for war, and took their places in the ranks with the century to which they belonged. Gradually, however, this organization came to have political significance, until finally these men, got together for what is the chief political duty in a primitive state, enjoyed what political privileges there were. As we have already seen, two of the most important functions of the *comitia curiata* had been the declaration of offensive war and the authorization of the wills of citizens, disposing of their property contrary to the *mos majorum*. It was so natural, that we can easily understand how both these matters passed from the control of the patricians' assembly to that of the army. Nothing could be more obviously just than that the men who were to fight the battles should decide whether the war was to be waged or not, and nothing more convenient than that the same men should have power to authorize the wills of their comrades which would be made in large numbers just before a fight. These two things paved the way for a general transfer of legislative functions, and in the end it became the rule for the magistrate to obtain consent in im-

portant things, not from the assembly of the *curiæ*, which met in the Forum, or on the Capitol, but from the army assembled without the walls, when all the soldiers voted by centuries, plebeians as well as patricians, and where not birth, but wealth and age, held the power. At the same time, the election of the subordinate military commanders, centurions and tribunes, devolved upon the soldiers, and to these positions any warrior was eligible. Of course, all this growth in power was very gradual. We must not look on it as a matter of years. Centuries may have been consumed in the transformation. We have no chronology of this early period by which to mark the flight of time. But in the end this *exercitus* of Servius Tullius formed another popular assembly, the *comitia centuriata*, which supplanted the *comitia curiata* entirely, except in matters connected with the religion of the family and very soon of purely formal significance. This organization, therefore, became of the highest civil importance, and was continued for civil purposes long after the army was marshaled on quite another plan.

4. **The Establishment of the Consular Government.**—The culmination in the power of the *comitia centuriata* was reached only after the monarchical form of government had been abolished. The last of the kings lost his position at the head of the state, as far as we can surmise from the legends, because he persistently violated the *mos majorum*, and pushed his exactions up to a point where retaliation became justifiable. His expulsion was

the work of the patricians exclusively, who proceeded to remodel the government after a pattern which should better secure to them political power. Henceforth, the priestly duties of the king were, at least in name, to be discharged by a new officer, the *rex sacrorum*, who was to hold his position for life. The civil duties of the king were given to two magistrates, chosen for a year, who were at first called *prætores* or "generals," *judices* or "judges," or *consules* (*cf. con* "together" and *salio* "to leap") or "colleagues." In the matter of their power, no violent departure was made from the *imperium* of the king. The greatest limitation on the consuls was the short period for which they were at the head of the state; but even here they were thought of, by a fiction, as voluntarily abdicating at the expiration of their term, and as nominating their successors, although they were required to nominate the men who had already been selected in the *comitia centuriata*. Another limitation was the result of the dual character of the magistracy. The *imperium* was not divided between the consuls, but each possessed it in full, as the king had before. When, therefore, they did not agree, the veto of the one prevailed over the proposal of the other, and there was no action. If no great interests were at stake, such mutual checks served a good purpose, because they saved the state from the dangers of mismanagement and usurpation. But, in times of emergency, there was need of greater vigor and decision in administration than could be expected from a double head. On such occasions, one of the consuls nominated a third "colleague," to whom both himself and his original colleague became subordinate.

5. **The Dictator and the Quæstors.**—This third colleague was called *dictator*, and on his accession he appointed as his assistant a "master of the horse" (*magister equitum*). His term of office expired with that of the consul who nominated him, and in any event was limited to six months. His power was quite extraordinary, as the king's had been, and, when contrasted with the consul's, shows what reductions, further than those already suggested, the supreme magistrate's rule had suffered by the abolition of the monarchy. The dictator was absolute both within and without the city, and from his judgment there was no appeal unless he chose to grant one. The consuls, on the other hand, were required to allow an appeal to the people, when capital or corporal punishment had been pronounced upon a citizen. This, of course, was a limit on their *imperium*. Again, when the dictator laid down his power, there was no tribunal before which he could be called to account for the way in which he had excrcised it. But the consuls, at the expiration of their term of office, were subject to legal prosecution, like any other citizens, for the misdemeanors of which they had been guilty. At the same time, the care and administration of the public treasury were transferred to two magistrates, who had been called into existence from time to time under the regal constitution at the convenience of the king. These were the so-called quæstors, who gained their name (original-

ly *quæstores parricidi*, "trackers of foul murder") from their earliest function of assisting the king in the detection of criminals. They now became regular officers in the city, exercising subordinate judicial powers, and acting as state treasurers.

**6. What the Plebeians gained by these Changes.**—Nothing could be further from the truth than to look on this change from monarchy to republic as due to anything like a popular uprising, such as has been made, now and again, in modern times, with the purpose of securing the control of the state to the governed. This struggle for the limitation of the magistrates' power was made entirely within the body of the patricians, and it was only indirectly that the plebeians were involved in it. In the dangers which threatened the state when the expelled kings took up arms in order to effect their restoration, the *plebs* had co-operated with the aristocracy against them. But the new government which was evolved out of this revolution was an aristocracy, which granted but few privileges to the crowd in return for their assistance. It seems clear, however, that at the close of the regal period the plebeians were admitted to membership in the *curiæ* and to votes in the *comitia curiata*. This made the *comitia curiata* a purely democratic assembly; but, as we have already seen, all its real powers had passed over to the *comitia centuriata*. Here, too, the plebeians had a voice, but, as the cavalry and the first class included ninety-eight of the one hundred and ninety-three centuries, the measures of the assembly were always decided by the richest citizens. The presence of the plebeians, however, in these legislative bodies, even in this subordinate way, was significant and valuable in their progress toward political equality. At this point, also, some of them gained admission to the senate, into the hands of which the control of the state was rapidly passing. In regal times, when the senate was acting in its capacity of adviser to the king, men who were not senators had sometimes been called in to assist in the deliberations. Now, at the beginning of the republic, some of these, among whom were some plebeians, were added permanently to the list of senators (*patres*). They were called *conscripti* ("added to the roll"), and were allowed to vote, though not to debate, when the matter before the senate was the giving of advice. The number of senators, however, including these *conscripti*, continued to be three hundred.

# CHAPTER V.

## THE FIGHT WITHOUT THE CITY.

1. **The Non-Italian Races of Italy.**—The people who inhabited Italy south of the Rubicon, at the dawn of history, were of three separate stocks, so far as language is an indication of race :

Calabria, and perhaps Apulia, was inhabited by a people whom the Greeks called Iapygians or Messapians. Their language, of which we learn a little from inscriptions found in Terra d' Otranto (the southeastern peninsula of Italy), is allied with the Latin and the Greek. They were probably the first of the Indo-European family to enter Italy.

In the northwest were the Etruscans or Tuscans, whose language—preserved only in inscriptions, mostly sepulchral, containing little more than names, and on a pair of ivory dice, on which the first six numerals can be read—has no undisputed connection with that of any branch of the Indo-European group. They entered Italy later than their neighbors, and took possession of the land around the Po, of Etruria proper, and afterward of the coast of the Volscian country and of northern Campania. In the beginning they surpassed the Italians in civilization and in military power.

2. **The Italian Races of Italy.**—The remaining peoples of Italy—the Umbrians, Sabines, Volscians, Oscans or Sabellians (which last is a name of convenience for the Samnites and their descendants), and the Latins—constitute linguistically so many branches of one family. The languages of the first four of these races, as far as they are known, resemble each other more closely than they do the Latins', from whom they seem to have separated in prehistoric times. These four are included together under the name of the Umbro-Sabellians. The Umbrians originally occupied the country to the north from sea to sea, but had been dispossessed of the western portion by the Etruscans. In the fourth century before Christ, the Senonian Gauls seized another strip bordering on the Adriatic, which was thenceforth called the Ager Gallicus. A hint about the structure of their language is given us by the so-called Eugubine Tables. South of the Umbrians, in the mountains of the interior, lived the Sabines, from whom were descended the inhabitants of Picenum, which was on the sea-coast, as well as the Vestini, the Marrucini, the Marsi, and the Peligni. No traces of their language are found, except in the Roman grammarians. The Volsci dwelt within the limits of what was afterward Latium, as did the Æqui, the Rutuli, the Hernici, and the Aurunci. On the evidence of inscriptions, the Volsci are closely related to the Umbrians. Concerning the languages of the others nothing is known. The Samnites held the inland country to the northeast of Campania.

Thence their descendants, the Frentani, spread eastward to the Adriatic. In the fifth century before Christ, the Samnites conquered Campania, and during the next half-century, Lucania and the Ager Bruttiorum. When Rome began its struggle with them for the hegemony of Italy, they held these districts and Apulia besides. Their language is known by us through inscriptions discovered in Apulia, Campania, and Samnium.

The Latins in the earliest time had probably held most of the lowlands from the Tiber to the southwestern extremity of the peninsula. From Cumæ southward, their nationality had succumbed to that of the Greeks, who, beginning perhaps in the eighth and ninth centuries before Christ, took possession of the Italian coast from Cumæ as far as Tarentum. At the dawn of their history, the Latins occupied a district of about seven hundred square miles, bounded by the Tiber, the Apennines, the Alban hills, and the sea.

3. **The Latin League.** — Among the clan-communities composed of these Latins dwelling in this limited territory, there had existed from time immemorial a confederation which, of course, included Rome. The basis of their union was their common language and religion, and it was designed for the purposes of defense against the common enemies of Latium—the Etruscans, who lived toward the north, and the Umbro-Sabellians of the mountains. This was the so-called "Latin League," in which, according to tradition, there were included thirty cantons. Alba Longa held the presidency, and

there an annual meeting of the league was held when the Latin games (*Latinæ feriæ*) were celebrated, and sacrifices made to the Latin god (*Jupiter Latiaris*). Alba Longa's position gave it no ruling power over the other members of the league. Each canton continued absolutely independent in its sovereign rights, while the league was capable of common action in its own name. This, together with the clan and the canton, makes the three political units of early Roman history. How the political power of the clans became lost in that of the cantons can only be conjectured. We know how the league grew into a state, because we know how Rome became mistress of Latium.

4. **The Conquest of Italy.**—None of the thirty cantons included in the Latin League were among those of her neighbors whom Rome reduced when she first essayed extending her borders by conquest. When she was confident of her strength, however, she took Alba Longa and usurped the presidency of the Latin League. This position, as has been said, primarily carried with it no political rights, but Rome's growing power converted it first into an hegemony, and finally into a sovereignty over the other members of the league. According to the terms of an alliance for offense and defense, which was made between Rome on the one hand and the Latin cities, which were not yet subdued, on the other, each party was to bear equally the burdens of any war which they might wage in common, and to share equally the fruits of victory. Rome, however, soon usurped the exclu-

sive right of declaring war and making peace on behalf of the league, and the exclusive command of the allied forces, and divided among her own citizens the lands of such colonies as were planted in conquered territory. The Latin cities submitted to these aggressions, both because they were no longer individually a match for Rome, and because collectively they needed the assistance of Rome in their struggles against their enemies in Italy and marauders from abroad. With powers thus proportioned, therefore, Rome and the Latin League began a series of successful wars against the Sabines on the east, who offered no serious resistance, and against the Volscians, the Hernicans and the Æquians, who lived within the limits of Latium. By 383 B. C. they had extended their dominion as far as the river Liris, the northern border of Campania, and assured their position by planting colonies which served as fortresses in the conquered country. Up to this time the Etruscans and the Greeks were the strongest people in Italy, and there are indications that, at the close of the regal period, the Etruscans subjected Rome and the Latins to a crushing defeat, and that this was followed by a short period during which Latium was, to some extent at any rate, under Etruscan domination. In the fourth century before Christ, however, the Etruscan power was materially weakened by the invasion of the Gauls and by wars which it carried on with the Syracusans and the Samnites. Etruria and the cities of Magna Græcia began, also, thus early to pay the penalty of their great prosperity, in the degeneracy of the national character which accompanied the spread of luxury.

**5. The Conquest of Italy** (*continued*).—As has already been said, the Campanians were Samnites by race, but they had lost sight of their descent, and were engaged in frequent wars with the Samnites of the mountains. In 343 B. C., during one of these wars, the Capuans offered to place their city under the control of Rome in exchange for aid against their enemies. Capua was at this time the second city of Italy in size and the first in wealth. When Rome accepted its proposition, the Latin towns broke into revolt. Roman aggression and the increased security of Latium had already weakened the bonds which held together Rome and the Latin League, and at least once before its members had taken up arms against the city. Now, when they became satisfied that Rome was about to enter upon an individual career of foreign conquest, and that this would increase her power out of all proportion to theirs, they united in a final effort to preserve their independence. Rome, however, gained the victory now as she had before. In 338 B. C. she dissolved the Latin League, and, with the design of isolating the Latin communities from each other, made individual treaties with them. By 326 B. C. she had completed the subjugation of Campania which she had begun when she occupied Capua, and here, as elsewhere, she confirmed her conquests by colonies. The Roman dominion now included the southern part of Etruria, which she had won soon after the Gallic invasion, Latium, Campania, and the Sabine country. All this was compacted into a strong and highly centralized empire with Rome at its head. B. C. 326 may be taken as the date when the Samnites began their great contest with this power for the hegemony of Italy. The extent of the Samnite territory at this time has already been given. In the wars which followed, all the nations of Italy, with the exception of the Greeks, were arrayed at one time or another against Rome, and when Rome triumphed, in 290 B. C., they all came under her power. In 280 B. C., Tarentum, in behalf of the Greek cities, called in the aid of Pyrrhus, King of Epirus, against the Romans. By 272 B. C. he had been defeated, Tarentum subdued, and Rome was mistress of Italy south of the Rubicon.

6. **The Greatness of Rome.**—The details of this very remarkable career of conquest have not been preserved to us in a shape which makes them easy or worthy of study. But a brief outline of the successive steps such as we have presented is valuable, both because it shows that the Romans must have been possessed of military skill and a capacity for governing of the highest order, and because it allows us to see by what agencies these qualities were developed to their perfection. There is no reason in the nature of things why the people of the town on the Tiber should have triumphed first over their neighbors in the lowlands and afterward over all Italy; and, when we sum up the advantages of its situation on the one side and its disadvantages on the other, they seem to neutralize each

other in a way which makes inferences quite impossible. Rome was built on a group of seven hills, and it was easier to fortify and defend such a position than the single hill on which most of the cantons about her had their citadels. But when she came to fight with the men of the mountains, like the Volscians and the Æquians and the Hernicans, her hundred or two feet of elevation above the level of the sea could not have counted for much in the contest. Her victory here and always must have been won because she was superior to her enemies in discipline, in perseverance, and in alertness. When once she had conquered them, moreover, she was able to attach them to herself and to hold them as part of her in a way that no other conquering power has ever done. In the case of those in her immediate neighborhood, the reason of this is to be found in the intelligence and fairness of her laws which made even partial rights of citizenship at Rome a prize worth striving for. And she secured the allegiance of those at a distance, because somehow she possessed the instinct of ruling with strength and justice such as to discourage revolt. Her capacities in these directions continued great through all her history. At the height of her power she was great in these three things: in her military system, her laws, and her government. The armies of the civilized and the barbarian world alike succumbed before her advance, as had the nations of Italy in these early years, and she consolidated her vast empire by such devices that its permanency was never threatened from within, and men forgot that they were Greeks or Gauls in the intensity of their devotion and loyalty to Rome as Romans. It is quite idle to speculate as to what it was which gave the Romans the pre-eminence over their neighbors in these qualities at the beginning, but these early wars and dealings with kinsmen and strangers around her, which we have recited, developed the powers of her people in all the lines where their strength lay. We can never hope to know how their strength came to lie in these directions, but the city's career gave them experience, and problems to solve, and the methods which they learned here were valuable when the field of their application became the world.

7. **What Rome learned in these Wars.**— Rome's early intercourse with her neighbors, for one thing, counted for much in the development of her legal system. Roman law is the proudest monument which is standing in our time to testify to the city's greatness. The judicial methods and principles of all the civilized nations of to-day are permeated through and through by ideas borrowed from Rome. A structure like this, which is to stand forever, was built slowly and by many hands. In the beginning, the city's commercial position must have given her a high appreciation of the value of law. A commercial people early acquire a regard for justice because they see that it pays. Men who trade and loan money profit, for example, by the enforcement of contracts. But law and justice are nowhere always the same, and in a primitive

community are very different indeed. We have already defined early law as a body of customs which have grown out of the decisions of chieftains on disputes submitted to them by their subjects. Its substance is custom, and justice is only its coloring. Before the local customs of Rome, however, had lost their flexibility so that they could not be altered, the city was thrown into intimate contact by commerce and war with people whose customs differed from hers. When she tried to meet them in a legal way, she had to throw aside much of what was arbitrary and peculiar in her own methods. Her customs and theirs, in as far as they were accidental, had in general nothing in common, but, in as far as they were embodiments of intelligence and justice, they coincided, because intelligence and justice are alike everywhere. In the attrition of their mutual dealings, therefore, the senseless formalism which characterizes most systems of early law was reduced, and a prominence given to simple principles of equity which are usually a quite subordinate element.

8. **What Rome learned in these Wars** (*continued*).—Rome also learned the rudiments of her subsequent skill as a ruling and consolidating power in her dealings with the subjugated Latins, and in the country of the Volscians and Æquians she founded her first military colonies which were to be fortresses to hold what she had won. This was the germ of her colonial system, by which she subsequently governed all Italy and finally the world. But, even with this device, she could never

have ruled with success the vast empire which she constructed, unless she had been willing to leave the administration of local affairs in each community to the local authorities. Rome, later in her history, became rapacious and extortionate in her treatment of her provinces, but she never interfered heedlessly with local institutions or superstitions. This is quite remarkable, because most conquering nations have tried to make proselytes of the conquered by force or persuasion. Rome, however, was tolerant of other peoples' customs and beliefs from the beginning, and one of the reasons was because she had never been isolated. Isolation makes men and nations unsympathetic, but Rome had been very familiar, before she became settled in her own ways, with the political and religious systems of the peoples which surrounded her. Those of the mountaineers must have borne a resemblance to hers, because she and they were of the same race, but with the Etruscans on the north it was very different. Their religion, for one thing, was a gloomy and cruel mysticism, very foreign to the practical common sense of the Romans. The knowledge that a great commercial nation like the Etruscans held such ideas, must have accustomed the Romans to strange things. Of course, this sort of experience was only one of many factors in the city's discipline, but it had its influence, as will appear when we consider in detail how Rome governed Italy.

9. **The Policy of Incorporation.** — Rome's policy at the beginning of her power was to in-

crease the number of her citizens in whatever ways she could. For this reason, she incorporated the inhabitants of the cantons which she first conquered, in the body of Romans as plebeians. Afterward, as treaties or conquest gave her opportunity, she did the same thing with the rest of the peoples in her vicinity, until most of the towns in the district bounded on the north by Caere, on the east by the Apennines, and on the south by the Formiæ, had become suburbs, as it were, of the Roman city. So long as the plebeians were denied their political rights, this incorporation was not looked on as a privilege by those who were forced to submit to it, because it made them a subject population in a foreign state. Before the time of the second Punic war, as we shall presently see, the plebeians had gained for themselves political equality, so that thenceforward all Romans in the region indicated, and previous to that, the patricians among them, were citizens with full rights. This territory was divided into tribes, which were made up after the analogy of the three original tribes from which the city had been formed. The number of these was increased as the limits of the incorporated territory were extended, until by 241 B. C. there were thirty-five. Four of them included the inhabitants of the city proper, and the other thirty-one those of the adjacent country. These tribes, as will be further noted, were entirely artificial organizations, made for convenience of governmental administration, and their members had no necessary relation to one another, either of blood or of common religion. Any man who was enrolled in any one of them had the right of going to Rome, in case he did not already live there, and of voting in the popular assemblies to which his rank admitted him (*jus suffragi*). He had also the right of holding political offices in the state (*jus honorum*), and the right of appealing to the people from any sentence which affected his life or his privileges as a citizen (*jus provocationis*). These were his public rights. He had also the private rights, the *jus commerci* and the *jus connubi*, which have been defined in another connection. Those who possessed thus both the public and private rights constituted the Romans proper, and in their hands during the continuance of the republic rested the government of the state.

10. **The Subject Communities of Italy.**—The subject communities in Italy—and there were none outside of Italy at this time—were of three classes. The first and most important were those which had the so-called Latin rights (*jus Lati* or *Latinitas*). Here were included some Latin towns like Tibur and Præneste, which Rome had not been strong enough to subject to incorporation, three Hernican towns whose faithfulness to Rome had been so uninterrupted that they had afforded no pretext for their incorporation, and the colonies which the city had planted as fortresses throughout the peninsula. The inhabitants of all these possessed the *jus commerci*, but generally not the *jus connubi*, and in the beginning the public rights were open to them under certain restrictions, provided they migrated

to Rome; but in the case of those colonies which were founded after 268 B. C., only the men who had held public magistracies in their own towns, acquired citizenship by settlement in the city. This class of subject communities enjoyed local self-government, and from it was drawn the main body of allies for the Roman army, known as "the allies of the Latin name" (*nomen Latinum*). The second class consisted of the so-called *præfecturæ*. These were some towns, like Caere in Etruria and Capua in Campania, whose distance from Rome was too great to warrant their incorporation in the city, and whose subjugation at the same time was too complete to win for them a place in the *nomen Latinum*. Their inhabitants were called *cives sine suffragio*, because, while they possessed the private, they were denied absolutely the public rights. They were subject, however, to all the burdens of Roman citizenship, and their local law was administered by prefects sent out from Rome. They occupied the least desirable position in the state. The third class included the Greek, Etruscan, and Umbro-Sabellian communities throughout Italy, which had been forced into treaties of perpetual alliance with Rome during the course of the long wars which she had waged for supremacy in the peninsula. The terms of these treaties varied with each community, but in general they were as liberal as was consistent with the position of the central city. Rome reserved to herself exclusively three functions only—declaring war, making treaties, and coining money. Local self-government was granted the allies, and exemption from direct taxation. All that was demanded of them was that they should each supply a fixed contingent to fight along with the Romans against the enemies of Italy.

11. **Rome's Colonial System.**—As far as the outside world was concerned, Italy was thus made one nation. Internally it was a compact confederacy, all the lines of which radiated from Rome as a center. The policy of incorporation had been pursued as far as was possible if Rome was to continue a city. Beyond this, the more remote communities, isolated politically from each other, were united to the capital as individuals. At the same time, Rome devoted herself earnestly and successfully to assimilating them to herself in their internal customs and institutions. The chief agents in this work were the Latin colonies, to which reference has already been made. These were called Latin, not because they were peopled by Latins, but because their inhabitants had the Latin rights (*jus Lati*). They ultimately numbered thirty-four, and were situated in all parts of the peninsula, from Ariminum in the country of the Gauls, to Brundisium in Calabria, and from Cales in Campania, on the west, to Firmum and Castrum Novum in Picenum on the east. Bodies of colonists were sent to them from Rome, varying in size according to the necessities of the regions in which they were founded. Four or five thousand was the usual number, but, at least in one instance, as many as twenty thousand were sent. These colonists were Roman citizens who were willing to suffer a diminution in their political

rights in return for the material advantages which they got from residence in these subject communities. They retained in their new homes their loyalty to Rome and the moral qualities which belonged to the Romans. Through their work the Italian dialects gave way to the Latin language, until Latin became the common Italian tongue. Through their presence, also, the Italian cities learned to model their governments after the pattern of Rome. At the same time, with their strong walls the colonies served admirably their original purpose of holding in subjection the conquered country.

12. **The Roman Roads.**—Beginning in 312 B. C., the Romans undertook to facilitate communication between Rome and the different parts of Italy by a system of military roads. The first of these, called the Via Appia, was built soon after the subjugation of Campania, and extended first to Capua, whence it was afterward continued through Venusia and Tarentum to Brundisium. Of the many others which were subsequently constructed, it is important to know about the Via Flaminia, which was built by 220 B. C., and, passing through Narnia and Fanum, terminated at Ariminum; about the Via Æmilia (B. C. 187), which connected Ariminum with Placentia; about the Via Valeria, which led through the country of the Sabines, Marsians, and Æquians; and about the Via Latina, which led through the valley of the Liris to Æsernia in Samnium. These roads were, for the most part, paved with blocks of hard stone placed above a foundation

two feet deep, and consisting of small stones and gravel. They were eighteen feet in width, and were raised a little in the middle for the purpose of drainage. They were constructed with the greatest care, and, in general, followed a straight line between the points which they connected. Mountains which stood in the way were penetrated by tunnels, streams were spanned by bridges, and marshes were crossed by viaducts of solid masonry. Over them it was possible to send a Roman army without any delay from difficulties of travel. Thus they served at once to further the work of assimilating Italy to Rome by spreading Roman ideas and to discourage anything like a concerted revolt on the part of the Italians. Of this last, however, there was no longer ground for fear. The Umbro-Sabellians had not yielded in their long struggle with Rome until their strength had been completely crushed. For them to take up arms against Rome, with its power grown and consolidated as has been described, would have been hopeless. In point of fact, they served faithfully in the united armies, making the number of men in Italy capable of bearing arms probably not much less than a million. It was a nation of this character which Hannibal tried to conquer with an army of twenty thousand foot and six thousand horse.

# CHAPTER VI.

## THE FIGHT WITHIN THE CITY.

**1. Primitive Ideas about Property.** — In primitive society, the right of the individual to own land was not recognized. The earliest stage of civilization was the pastoral, and then, of course, men moved from place to place as their flocks and herds needed pasture and water. When they began to till the soil, since land was plenty and the laborers few, the site of their settlement was constantly shifted, and they brought rich new fields under cultivation after each harvest to take the place of those impaired by use. It was clearly quite inconsistent with either of these systems that an individual should hold as his own any particular section of land to the exclusion of his fellows. In the pastoral stage, no thought was given to the soil except for the grass which grew on it, and even when agriculture had become a common pursuit among men, the crop was the great thing—the land was boundless and anybody's. The methods inherited from these times continued after the community had abandoned the nomadic life in all its forms, and settled once for all in a limited and circumscribed territory. The arable fields were cultivated in common by all the citizens, and the harvested crops divided among the laborers man by man. The waste land was held as pasture, and here was the general grazing-ground for all the flocks and herds owned in the community. When the population increased by natural means and by the combination of clans, parts of this system were outgrown. Sections of the arable domain were then assigned to families. These they were to cultivate in common, as the community had cultivated the whole at the beginning. This land was not regarded as the property of the family to which it was given, but was theirs simply to use, and that, too, for a limited period. At fixed intervals they were required to turn it into the common stock for redistribution.

2. **The Land System of the Romans.**—At the dawn of Roman history, all of these stages had already been passed through, and the right of private ownership in real estate was well established. We can picture the community at the outset as living under a common roof, but now every *pater familias* owned in fee a small piece of land (*heredium*) around the family tomb, large enough for his house and garden. He could neither sell nor devise this, because it had originally come to him as a temporary grant from the state, and because it was sacred as the site of the family's altar. As families enlarged and divided, each new *pater familias* was given a similar *heredium* out of the community's domain. This was not exactly the same thing as owning land, but it accustomed men's minds to the idea that there might be the same sort of property

in the soil as there was in other things.  The *heredium*, however, was of course not sufficient for the support of the family, and the main reliance must still have been on the common property of the state, which was farmed out to the citizens for limited periods.  The state finally failed, from one cause or another, to reclaim the land which had been assigned for occupation, until each occupant came to view that which he held as his own.  When he was allowed to alienate this during his life and to dispose of it at his death by will, all the features of the modern systems of land tenure appeared at Rome.  The details of this transition are entirely unknown to us, but, if the traditions about the classification of the people by Servius Tullius on the basis of their property have any foundation in fact, individual ownership of land must have been very general at Rome at a very early time.

3. **The Lands acquired in War.** — The state's domain, however, was constantly extending along with its success in war.  In primitive times, after a military victory, the discipline of the army was suspended, the soldiers were dismissed from the ranks with free license to plunder the enemy, and the movable property of the conquered became the spoil of the victor to seize and carry off at his will.  By an extension of this custom, when Rome subdued a state, she not only succeeded at once to the possession of its public works, treasures, and revenues, but also became absolute owner of the land which had belonged to its inhabitants in severalty, so far as this system prevailed.  The severity

with which she exercised this power varied with the completeness of her victory and the objects which she had in view. But, in general, she granted back part of the territory which she thus acquired to the men from whom she had taken it. The rest of it was hers, and she had to make some disposition of it. In the earliest time, we can conceive of her as holding it for the common use of her citizens, and, later, as renting it for a nominal sum or parceling it out to them in fee. When the plebeians began to fight in the armies, it became the custom to assign that part of the conquered land which was arable in equal portions to the men who had won it with their arms, citizens and non-citizens, to hold as their individual property. That which was not arable was reserved as a common pasture-ground, for the use of which a small grazing-tax was exacted. Strictly the patricians alone, from the beginning, enjoyed this privilege of pasturing their cattle on the state's land; but, while the regal constitution continued, the royal indulgence had extended it to the plebeians also. This was because, in the inevitable struggles between the sovereign and the aristocracy, which occur in every absolute monarchy, the Roman kings had found the *plebs* valuable allies, and there is more than one trustworthy tradition that they had tried to bring them within the pale of political privileges in return for their support.

4. **The State's Lands under the Consular Government.**—But when the rule of the aristocracy began, on the expulsion of the kings, the ple-

beians lost whatever had thus been secured to them. The patricians became in deed as well as in name the exclusive tenants of the common pasture-grounds. At the same time, the divisions of the arable land, in which all the warriors had shared, were abandoned for the most part, and in their place was revived the primitive system of distribution (*occupatio*), which had been in use when the plebeians were but a small factor in the state. By this the state henceforth retained the ownership of the arable, as it had of the pasture lands in the past; and, in return for a fixed annual rental, granted them in portions to individuals to hold and transmit to their heirs, subject always to the right of the state to resume possession at its pleasure. This change in the disposition of the public lands began at once to work mischief, and finally led to all the agrarian troubles which wrecked the Roman state. At the very outset, the partiality of the magistrates, who had charge of the distribution, limited it to their immediate circle of patricians and rich plebeians. Again, the collection of the rentals, as well as of the grazing-tax, devolved on the quæstors. But they were patricians, appointed to office by the consuls, who, in turn, were elected in the *comitia centuriata*, where wealth held the power. Naturally enough, therefore, out of devotion to their caste, they were negligent in this part of their duty, until these rents soon ceased to be paid at all, and the occupation of the arable lands came to differ from their ownership only in name. Finally, the revenues of the state, which would have been fully adequate had this source of income been available, fell so far short of its needs that it was necessary to resort constantly to the imposition of the *tributum* to supply the deficiency. But all the freeholders had been made subject to this by the Servian constitution.

5. **The Early Agrarian Troubles.**—The poor land-holders were in this way subjected to the burdens of increased taxation, while, at the same time, their incomes were diminished by the competition of the large farms of the patricians, which already began to be worked by gangs of slaves. No small part of them, too, were tenants of the rich. Some were hereditary clients, whose whole stock in trade was derived from their patrons. Some, who belonged to the other classes of plebeians, had been forced to lease property from the owners of large estates, because they could get none for themselves from the state by way of assignment or of occupation. But all of these had rents to meet, for which the returns from their farms were now often inadequate. The poor, who were largely plebeians, became thus the debtors of the rich—the freeholders, for money borrowed, and the tenants because they could not discharge their obligations to them. But in ancient Rome the creditor looked for his debt to the person of his debtor, not to his property. If the debtor failed to pay what he owed on the day appointed, he was seized and confined for sixty days. If at the end of that time no one had come to his rescue, he could be sold into slavery, or put to death, at the option of his creditors. It is obvi-

ous that a plebeian, when he had once become involved in debt, would find it very difficult to save himself from these extreme consequences; and, in point of fact, the traditions from this period tell us that the poor plebeians passed in large numbers into bondage to their wealthy fellow-citizens. It was along this line that the next great battle in Rome's constitutional development was fought. While, without, the field was Italy and Roman arms were victorious in every quarter, within, the lines were closely drawn for a conflict of another nature. It is important to notice that the combatants were not the patricians and the plebeians, but the rich on the one side against the poor on the other. The subject of dispute was not an abstract question of political rights, but it concerned the material interests and physical comfort of the commonalty. It was only because these would be furthered by the political equality of the two orders in the state that they aimed at this.

6. **The Tribunes of the Plebs.**—The first movement in the struggle was the secession of the *plebs* to the Sacred Mount in 494 B. C., and the consequent institution of the plebeian tribuneship. Two new officers were thus created in the state who were to be elected by the plebeians in an assembly by *curiæ*. Like the consuls they held office for a year only, but their power was of the most unusual and extensive character. The general object of their appointment was that the plebeians might find in them protectors against the rapacity and injustice of their oppressors. For this purpose, they were

empowered to interfere with any magistrate in the discharge of the duties of his office where the interest of any individual plebeian was concerned. They could, for example, save a citizen from the military levy, or rescue an insolvent debtor from the hands of his creditors. But, on the other hand, they were powerless against the *imperium* of the consul, when outside the city at the head of his army, and against that of the dictator both within and without the city. Nor could they, in the beginning, veto any legislative or judicial act as a whole, but they were limited to securing exemption for individuals from its operation. Wider powers in this respect were afterward obtained for them, but this restriction at the outset made the work of their office too great for two men to discharge, and their number was early increased to five, and afterward to ten. There was the more need for this change, because they had added to their original functions a jurisdiction in judicial proceedings. This seems to have been a pure usurpation on their part, but it soon became one of the most considerable of their duties, in the discharge of which they were assisted by two new officers, the plebeian *ædiles*.

7. **The Concilium Tributum Plebis.**—An appeal was granted from any sentence pronounced by a tribune, in his capacity of judge, to the curiate assembly of plebeians which had elected him, just as an appeal from the consul's decision was had to the people in the *comitia centuriata*. Before this assembly the tribune had the right to explain and defend the course which he had taken, and the plebeians,

after hearing him, passed resolutions of indorsement or dissent (*plebiscita*). When the tribunes had got the *plebs* together for this purpose, there were a thousand questions of another character which it occurred to them from time to time to discuss in their presence. On these, too, the plebeians used to express their opinion by votes which were binding as far as they concerned themselves alone. But in the beginning, they had, of course, no more power to legislate for the entire community by such resolutions than would any irregular meeting of citizens in modern times. In 471 B. C., however, by the Publilian law, the constitution and powers of the plebeian assembly were radically changed. In the first place, the arrangement by *curiæ*, which had prevailed during its first twenty years, now gave way to a tribal organization. When Servius had formed his new *exercitus*, he had divided the city into four artificial tribes, for convenience in making the levy. In 495 B. C., seventeen further divisions of the same character were made in the incorporated country about the city. The law of Publilius provided that every plebeian freeholder who was enrolled in any one of these twenty-one tribes should have the right to vote in a new legislative assembly, the "*concilium tributum plebis,*" in which the plebeian tribunes and ædiles were to be elected. The object of this reform is said by Livy to have been to prevent the patricians from exercising a control over the measures of the commonalty as they had been able to through their clients while the arrangement by *curiæ* was maintained. At the same time, it is conjectured, the *plebiscita* were made binding on the state at large, like the laws of the *comitia centuriata*, provided they had previously received the sanction of the whole senate.

8. **How the Tribuneship worked in Practice.**—There have been a great many absolute monarchs in modern times, but, as we have already remarked, none exactly like the Roman *rex;* and in the same way, although there have been a great many constitutional struggles in modern times, the combatants in no one of them have ever thought to compromise by creating a magistracy like the Roman plebeian tribuneship. In fact, this office is quite without parallel in the history of any other nation, and it is one of the many evidences which we have of the early Romans' ability to exercise unusual powers with moderation that the orderly development of the Roman system of government was materially assisted by its existence. But, even they themselves were harassed by its obvious inconveniences. Here were officers, elected by a part of the people, originally intended to be protectors of the poor, who had so extended their functions that in civil matters they stood on a level with the consuls in the initiation and execution of public business, and besides were able to practically stop the wheels of government, at their will, by interposing their veto. There were thus two hostile cities with all the machinery of government in full operation, living together and within each other. Both orders in the state recognized the dangers and difficulties of such a state of affairs, and united in concessions

which would remove the necessity for its continuance. From a political standpoint, this was the occasion for the institution of the decemvirate in 451 B. C. It was hoped that if the laws of the state, which had thus far been a matter of oral tradition in the hands of the few, were codified and published, so as to be accessible to the poor and unlearned as well as to the rich and noble, sufficient protection could be secured for the plebeians without the existence of the tribuneship.

9. **The Decemvirate.**—With this end in view, the regular consular and tribunician government was temporarily supplanted by a commission of ten men elected by the *comitia centuriata*. They were clothed with complete executive power, even the right of appeal from their decisions being suspended. At the same time, they formed what would correspond in some degree to a constitutional convention of modern times. Their sphere here, however, was wider than that of a constitutional convention, because the criminal and civil as well as the public law came within their cognizance. In general, they were to collect and amend the laws of Rome until their definitions and provisions should be an efficient substitute for the practical anarchy to which tribunician interference every now and then gave rise. Plebeians were made eligible to this office. We have not yet at this period emerged from the darkness and obscurity which cover the early history of the city, and we can not feel any confidence that the accounts which the ancients give us of the decemvirate are at all

trustworthy. The story that the decemvirs were driven out of power by a popular uprising is now generally disbelieved, and it is taken to be much more likely that they were not allowed to complete their work because they had incurred the hostility of the aristocracy by the liberal provisions which they made for the plebeians' protection. The code which they compiled under the name of the laws of the Twelve Tables has been preserved to us only in a mutilated condition, but our information about it from all sources is very considerable. Its immediate effect on the pending constitutional struggle was very great, and it had a subsequent influence of the most wide-reaching character on the development of Roman law.

10. **The Influence of the Decemvirate's Legislation on the Development of Roman Law.**—To consider these points in an inverse order, it is to be noticed that many advantages naturally followed from the codification of the law at so early a stage in its history. It was by this means reduced to a simple and intelligible form, capable of application in a wide range of cases, before the more extended business interests of the city had given it a complexity which would make this difficult, if not impossible. Unless, however, a legal system have in it the principle of growth, there is a danger in such early codification which may outweigh its benefits. It may happen that strange and hard problems will present themselves, and that the code, which is supposed to contain all the law, can furnish no solution, because it was

compiled when such a complication could not have been thought of. But Roman ingenuity guarded by many devices against this serious difficulty, and kept its laws replete with life and adapted to meet each new combination of circumstances. One of these devices involved constant reference to the laws of the Twelve Tables, and made them the real or feigned source of much of what was purest and most intelligent in the city's legal system. In this respect, they came to hold the same relation to the general Roman law as the common law does to that of England. In the view of the English courts, there could arise in the realm no case not covered by statute, which was not adequately provided for in the mass of customs and precedents constituting in theory the common law of the land. If in any instance the principle of no previous decision could be made to fit, the judge found guidance, as it was said, *in nubibus*. In other words, he legislated for the case, drawing on his own sense of justice and enlightened judgment for the law which would be applicable. At Rome, in the same way, there grew up a class of lawyers (*jurisconsulti*) whose knowledge of the contents of the Twelve Tables was relied on as final. At first this was a matter of irregular custom, but under the empire it was controlled by statutes. When a case came before him, the judge, who may have been quite unlearned in such things, having ascertained the facts, asked a *jurisconsultus* for information about the provisions of the code which covered it. Quite usually it contained no provisions which had any reference to the matter, because, of course, society soon developed situations much beyond the ken of men like the decemvirs, who lived four hundred years or more before Christ. But, under these circumstances, the *jurisconsultus* invented an equitable disposition of the subject under dispute, and reported it as though he had found it in one of the Twelve Tables. This did not deceive any one; but, by a legal fiction, the solution necessary for every problem was supposed to be in the code, and the *jurisconsulti* to be capable of finding it. These lawyers, thus, on the basis of this early legislation, became one of the great agents in maintaining the freshness and adequacy of the Roman laws. They were practically legislators, but always with reference to this simple system of the decemvirs.

11. **The Political Effect of the Decemvirate's Legislation.**—The decemvirate passed out of existence in 449 B. C., but its legislation was incorporated into the constitution of the state by a decree of the people made in the *comitia centuriata*. The ill-defined powers of the patrician consuls were, therefore, limited by its work, as had been the intention of all parties concerned, at the time of its creation. But, in spite of this fact, the tribunate, which had proved such a hindrance to the easy course of the government, was restored, with all the extraordinary prerogatives attached to it, unimpaired except in one particular. This, of course, was a very important gain for the plebeians, and is an indication that their power in the state was now so formidable that their ultimate success in the

struggle for political equality was assured. The peculiar reasons which had originally led to the institution of the tribunate, however, ceased to be operative because the poor no longer stood in constant need of political protectors when the laws were known, and the discriminations which they had unjustly made in favor of the rich had been repealed. The character of this plebeian magistracy began, therefore, at this period to undergo considerable change. The power which the tribunes had usurped, of vetoing a decree of the senate as a whole instead of securing exemption for individuals from its operation, and the right which the plebeian assembly where they presided had acquired of legislating for both orders in the state, made it seem advisable to give them seats in the senate. It was simply a waste of labor for the senate to devise measures if some tribune was to veto them afterward, and this could be prevented only by having what objections there were, stated in advance. The tribunes in this way listened and were heard in the debates in the *curia*. When their opposition could not be removed, no attempt was made to mature any proposition under consideration; and, on the other hand, they were constantly relied on by the senate to carry through the *concilium plebis* measures which the senate was interested in having enacted. At the best period of the Roman republic, therefore, the plebeian tribunes were attached to the senate, instead of being protectors of the poor. This complete transformation was not made until a much later time, and will be discussed more fully in another connection; but its beginning dates from the restoration of the office after the administration of the decemvirs.

12. **The Consular Tribunes.**—At this point, one further temporary change was made in the form of government, which was significant for many reasons, but for one in particular. As has been pointed out, the combatants thus far in this constitutional struggle at Rome were the rich, plebeians and patricians, on the one side, against the poor on the other. But, four years after the abolition of the decemvirate (445 B. C.), a law was enacted which put the *imperium* into the hands of officers who might by the constitution be chosen as well from among the plebeians as from the patricians. These were the so-called consular tribunes. Instead of electing two consuls who should appoint six military tribunes to command the legions under them, as had been the custom, it was now provided that the people might elect six or a smaller number of *tribuni militum*, and confer on them the power which the consuls had exercised (*imperium consulare*). As all the soldiers, both plebeians and patricians, had been considered eligible to the military tribuneship, plebeians might now obtain the consular power, though not yet the consulate itself. With the *imperium* thus in their grasp, the plebeian aristocracy were induced to recognize the fact that there was a practical community of interests between themselves and the less prosperous members of their own class. The institution of the consular tribuneship was in this way of the utmost impor-

tance, because it led to an alliance between the rich and poor plebeians. The two orders in the state were now clearly marked, and every year they tested their strength in a struggle over the question whether the consular government should be restored or not. When the patricians won, they held the chief magistracies, of course, exclusively; and at first, even in those years when consular tribunes were chosen, the patricians succeeded in filling the whole number from among themselves. But there could be no doubt about the final result of this contest, now that the plebeians were united.

13. **The Military Quæstor, the Censor, the Prætor, and the Curule Ædile.**—In 367 B. C., the consulship, now permanently re-established, was thrown open to the plebeians by the Licinian laws. It was further provided by the same measure that one at least of the consuls should always be a plebeian, while both might be selected from that order. The patricians, however, in expectation of this outcome, had already succeeded in making a considerable reduction in the consuls' power. We have seen how the care of the city's treasures had been intrusted to two city quæstors, soon after the abolition of the monarchy. In like manner, soon after the fall of the decemvirate, the expenditures connected with military affairs, which had hitherto been in the hands of the consuls, were put under the control of new patrician officers, the military quæstors, who were to accompany the army on its march. They were to be elected in the *comitia tributa,* an assembly of the whole people,

patricians as well as plebeians, by tribes. Of this we now hear for the first time. If it had any previous history it is unknown by us, but the right of legislating was secured to it by a law of this same date (449 B. C.). In 435 B. C., the censorship was established. Its functions were very extensive, and made the most serious inroad on the consul's *imperium*. The censor made a list of all the citizens, once in five years, and a register of each man's property. On the basis of one or the other or both of these, he assigned to every one his position in the different popular assemblies. In addition, he had among the executive officers the ultimate control over the state's finances, so far as the collection of its revenues was concerned, and over such expenditures as were connected with the construction of public works, roads, bridges, buildings, and the like. Immediately after the enactment of the Licinian laws, the prætorship and the curule ædileship were instituted. The reason given in the first case was the alleged ignorance of the plebeians about the law, and a field was provided for the new office by stripping the consuls of the jurisdiction which they had had in judicial matters. There were to be two curule ædiles, and to them was given the supervision of the markets and public works, together with police judicial powers necessary for its exercise. But all these offices, and the dictatorship in addition, were opened to the plebeians by the year 337 B. C.

14. **The Greater Gods of the Romans.**— Side by side with the magistrates who exercised

political functions in the state, there was a great body of officials who were concerned primarily with the care of the national religion. Some of these priesthoods had existed from the earliest times, and others had been created as the character of the state's civil constitution or its worship had been altered; but they were all, at the outset, occupied exclusively by the patricians, as a matter of course. From these positions, moreover, they were not so easily dislodged. The gods in the Roman system and the popular ideas about their nature had expanded very greatly before the time of the second Punic war, from the form in which we have pictured them in a preceding chapter. This was partly the result of internal development, and partly due to intellectual contact with the Greeks. The second of these influences was, however, in every way much the more important. We have seen how completely the Romans carried out one species of god-making, but their success in this direction was offset by their comparative incapacity for independent growth in the other line. They assigned to every object in their world its special deity, but were quite unequal to the work of detaching these special deities from the things to which they had originally belonged and converting them into gods. The Greeks, whose heritage of ideas from the Indo-European stock is taken to have been the same as that of the Romans, quickly filled an Olympus with a great throng of divinities of man-like natures. Their gods were soon transferred from the narrow activities in which they exercised themselves at their birth, and were fancied as possessing undefined powers in all directions. They became, as it were, another race of beings, more glorious than men, dwelling in a world more glorious than men's world, but having human passions and ambitions. The story of their lives and mutual relations was told and believed as one might tell and believe the history of a city on the earth, in which were recounted the deeds of heroes, the sorrows which come from love, and bits of personal description, gossip, and scandal. The explanation of this is found in the brightness of the Greek mind and the vigor of its imagination. But the Romans, as long as they remained intellectually isolated, never developed a mythology. They had their inherited conception of Jupiter and of Vesta, as divinities of a general character. But, with these exceptions, they clung with persistency to the worship of the many *numina* of various things, as already described. They selected, however, from among these for especial honor, those of them which were the doubles of things exceptionally important in their lives. Thus *Mars*, "the spirit of killing," was worthy of attention from a warlike people, and under this name, or as *Quirinus*, the corresponding Sabine deity, he was signaled out for general worship, because "he hurled the spear, protected the flocks, and overthrew the foe." In the same way, *Terminus*, the "spirit of boundaries," *Ceres*, the "spirit of growth," *Pales*, the "spirit of the flocks," *Saturnus*, the "spirit of sowing," *Janus*, the "spirit of opening," and others like them, became general gods in whose worship there was a national and periodic participation. Even these, however, were not, like the Greek gods, completely anthropomorphized and endowed with general powers. No tales were told of their exploits. They were like the others, except that the character of the things with which they were connected, like *sowing*, or the frequency of their occurrence, like *opening*, gave them pre-eminence and universal importance.

**15. The Greek Modifications of the Roman Religion.**—The infusion of Greek ideas about theology wrought great changes in this system. We have no definite information as to when this was made or in what manner. It must have come, of course, from the Greek cities in Italy, because there are no evidences of intimacy between Rome and Greece proper in this early time. But we can no more hope to know its details than we can hope to know the details of the introduction of the alphabet into Rome, which was part of the same general movement. The Romans met the Greeks of Magna Græcia in trade and arms. They learned with interest of their ability to extract from the gods information and guidance by means of oracles and sacred writings. They purchased from the men of Cumæ the Sibylline books to be used in this way, and, from what they learned there and from what Greeks told them, they began to supplement their catalogue of gods and to alter their nature. The guiding principle in this transformation was the idea that, for every Greek god, there existed or should exist a corresponding one of their own.

This notion was probably based on the ease with which apparent identification was effected in many cases; but, when once begun, difficulties and contradictions were not allowed to stand in the way of its thorough application. The debt in every case was from the Roman to the Greek. *Jupiter* and *Mars*, having some attributes in common with those of *Zeus* and *Ares*, were endowed with all the qualities which the Greeks had given to these creatures of their fancy. In other cases, a mere accidental resemblance was counted sufficient to justify identification and all which it implied. Thus, *Saturnus*, the god of sowing, was identified with *Kronos* simply because he was reputed to be of great antiquity, and then was made the father of *Jupiter* because *Kronos* was the father of *Zeus* in the Greek legends. Where gods were lacking for the purposes of this identification, *numina* were elevated to the rank of gods. *Minerva* (*cf. mens*), the spirit or double of mental power, was in this way made to correspond with the great Greek goddess *Athene*, and *Mercurius* (*cf. merx*), the spirit or double of trade, was conceived to be the same as the clever *Hermes*, the messenger of the gods. Finally, whenever the limitless number of *numina* suggested no parallel, the Greek gods themselves were directly transferred with their histories and characters intact. Thus, for example, *Apollo* and *Hercules* and *Castor* and *Pollux* came to be worshiped at Rome.

16. **The Value of this Transformation.**—All this had been accomplished by the time of the second Punic war. It appears to have been quite

gradual in its progress, and to have been, on the whole, beneficial as far as it had any influence at all. The Greek's conception of the divine nature was higher than the Roman's, and men's lives are shaped and colored in great measure by the character of their ideas on such matters. If they are not capable of developing themselves, the infusion of stimulating notions from outside will be valuable provided these can be assimilated. The Romans thus got enough from the Greeks in this early time to give some warmth to their own worship, but much of what they adopted in name was quite without effect in practice, because it was so foreign. The Roman's religion by itself was purely a matter of faith and ceremony. In the first place, he believed that there were gods who had power over men; and, in the second place, he propitiated them by the exact performance of such rites as he thought they demanded. It was entirely different from religion in the modern sense, which includes moral and theological elements. There was little connection between morality and religion among the Romans, and their minds shrank from debates about the nature of God, with which theology concerns itself. When contact with the Greeks would have carried them into these fields, they long failed to follow. During the years of their growth their religion of action was the worship of the doubles of their dead, and of such things as had influence on their lives. As already said, the city, like the family, had its ancestors, and their honor was maintained against intruders from within and enemies from without.  The struggle between the so-called patricians and plebeians got more than half its earnestness from the unwillingness of the former to admit strangers to participation in the sacrifices to their dead.  As the plebeians, however, forced their way to political equality, this early faith lost its intensity along with its exclusiveness.  The family worship, and that of the state, modeled after it, were still maintained, but the general views which came from the Greeks were getting the ascendency.

17. **The Priesthoods.**—The priestly office of the king had been delegated, at the beginning of the republic, to a *rex sacrorum*, but his sphere was limited to the offering of sacrifices, while all the sacred powers of the king were in the hands of the *pontifex maximus*.  He may be described as the head of the state's religious system during the historical period.  From the earliest times there had existed at Rome a college of pontiffs, who held their positions for life, and were the repositories of the nation's sacred lore.  When the regal constitution came to an end, they chose for themselves a head who should perform such duties as needed the services of one person, and which had before been performed by the king.  This *pontifex maximus* lived in the *regia*, close by the *atrium* of the city where was burning its sacred fire.  He selected the vestal virgins who tended this flame, and appointed the priests (*flamines*) on whom rested the care of honoring particular deities.  Of these there was a large number, but three were particularly important, the priest of *Jupiter* (*Flamen Dialis*), and

the priests (*flamines*) of *Mars* and *Quirinus*. The *pontifex maximus* also, in company with the other pontiffs, interpreted the laws of religion, and acquired enormous political influence in this way. No movement could be made in any department of the government which it was not in his power to arrest by declaring it to be in violation of the state's religion. When he did not care to interfere in this direct style, however, he could exert the same pressure by altering the calendar, for the regulation of this rested in his hands, or by the character of the answer which he gave, when consulted as to the proper course of procedure in a court or popular assembly—a matter about which he was supposed to have exclusive knowledge. A similar political influence was exercised by the augurs and the keepers of the Sibylline books, one or the other of whom was consulted before any public measure of importance was undertaken. The augurs, of whom there was a college, and who, like the pontiffs, held office for life, declared whether the gods favored or opposed any proposed enterprise by observing the heavens or the flight of birds, and the keepers of the Sibylline books by interpreting and expounding these sacred writings. So long as the patricians alone held these positions, to the exclusion of the plebeians, no matter how complete an equality was established in respect to the civil offices, the real political power of the two orders was quite different. It was possible for the patricians through the agency of the augurs to prevent the election of magistrates, or their entering on their duties after their election, or the holding of a popular assembly which was likely to pass a law obnoxious to them, simply by having the augurs declare the auspices unfavorable to proceeding. The plebeians never made any effort to secure admission to such priesthoods as were of a purely religious character, and the patricians always retained the sole right of eligibility to the position of the *flamines*, and of the *rex sacrorum*, and to the college of the *Salii* who worshiped Mars by dancing. But the prize connected with the priesthoods which were of political importance was too great to be the exclusive property of one order. By the Licinian laws, the number of guardians and interpreters of the Sibylline books was increased from two to ten, and plebeians made eligible to the office; and by the Ogulnian law of 296 B. C. the number of pontiffs, as well as that of the augurs, was increased from six to nine, and the plebeians obtained the right to five of the nine places in each college.

18. **The End of the Struggle.**—The end of the long struggle between the two orders was reached in the Hortensian law, passed about 287 B. C. By this a *plebiscitum* was freed from all limitations, and a decree of the *plebs*, made under the guidance of a tribune, rendered as binding over the whole people without the approval of the senate as a decree of the *comitia centuriata*, made under the guidance of a consul. The accounts which the ancient authorities give us of this measure make it seem identical with the one already enacted in connection with the institution of the *concilium plebis*. Some modern writers, therefore, regard it as sim-

ply a re-enactment of an earlier law which had not been observed; while others suppose that up to this time the control of the senate had been greater over the legislation of the *plebs* than over that of the *populus*, and that they were now placed on an equality in this particular. In any event, however, the tables were turned on the patricians in the matter of political disability. The plebeians were members of every popular assembly, and were eligible to every office and to every influential priesthood. The patricians had no votes in an assembly in which very many of the most important laws were passed, were not eligible to the powerful office of tribune of the *plebs*, or to the office of plebeian ædile, and were excluded from one consul's and one censor's position, while the plebeians were legally eligible for both.

19. **The Economic Results of the Struggle.**—As we look back over the conflict thus ended, it wears the aspect of a senseless scramble for offices, without any regard to the acquisition of more substantial advantages. It had begun in discontent, based on the exclusion of the poor from rights before the law which made their lot harder to bear, and their poverty greater. Leaving out the religious motive, the patricians resisted the efforts of the plebeians to force their way into the administration of the state, because they enjoyed the exercise of power, and because it secured them privileges and immunities which were valuable. The intensity of the plebeians' ambition for political equality, on the other hand, increased with their success, and this,

which had been desired at first only because of the material good it carried with it, became soon the main object of their endeavors. The aristocracy yielded with infinite cleverness inch by inch, and used to their uttermost the advantages which the best always have in a contest with the many. Where the commonalty grasped for a reality, it humored them with the gift of a name; and in the end, when they had got all the offices which they ought for, the real prize of the battle was still unwon. The Licinian laws, which opened the consulship, contained in addition provisions for a more equitable division of the public lands, and for the relief of the debtor class. But such laws were enacted more easily than they were enforced, and in this instance remained so many words in the statute-books. The state's progress in war and the expansion of its commerce diverted the minds of the poor from their unfortunate situation, but no remedy was forthcoming for it until the Gracchi devised one which wrecked the constitution. In spite, however, of the insubstantial character of these movements from one standpoint, they were very real from some others.

20. **The Social Results of the Struggle.**—They destroyed forever the old patriarchal form of the city's government, and supplanted its simplicity by a system which was complex and full of refinements. The powers of the king, for example, which the early consuls had inherited, were now in the hands of a group of officers whose original unity no one but an antiquarian could see. The

integrity of the family organization, too, was loosened as the worship of the household gods declined and Greek notions increased in popularity. The line which had divided the citizens from the crowd was obliterated, and legal marriages were contracted between members of the two orders. The sacred ceremony (*confarreatio*) by which they had been solemnized, gave way to civil forms. The individual got greater power over the disposition of his property, and new sorts of wills were invented for this purpose which should not require the cumbersome formalities of the old one. The limits of kinship were extended widely enough to admit all those whom ordinary natural affection would include, and the blood of cognates was made as good for the purposes of inheritance as was the blood of those who could trace their descent through males. The agent in these innovations was the prætor, who had the right of legislating by means of an edict issued at his entrance to office. He, however, only acted in response to popular opinion, which demanded that the artificialities of the earlier system should come to an end. The ancient city in its essential features perished, therefore, in this contest, and that which emerged from it was, to all intents, modern in its structure. The old ways of looking at things, however, had their influence still for a long time, just as men who change their faith or their environment frequently act and think, in spite of their desire to the contrary, according to their former creed or surroundings which they supposed they had left forever.

# CHAPTER VII.

## HOW ROME WAS GOVERNED AT THE TIME OF THE SECOND PUNIC WAR.

1. **The Nobilitas.**—The natural inference from this very complete triumph of the plebeians is that the government evolved out of the struggle would be a democracy, and such the facts already stated show that it was, at least in theory. But, in its actual operation, it maintained its aristocratic character until the time of the Gracchi. The rule of the patrician aristocracy, which had begun at the abolition of the monarchy, terminated with the passage of the Licinian laws, opening the consulship to the plebeians. Immediately after it the control of the state began to settle in the hands of the *nobilitas*. The *nobilitas* was, from the outset, an aristocracy, which differed from the patriciate, not in its nature, but in its composition. As we have seen, to be a patrician one had to be a descendant of some member of a clan contained in the three original Roman tribes. The *nobilitas*, on the other hand, was an aristocracy composed of the descendants of office-holders. Any man, any one of whose ancestors had held a curule office, was from this fact a noble. The curule offices, in the order in which

they were held, were the curule ædileship, the prætorship, the consulship, and perhaps the censorship, or, in general, those whose duties and privileges had, under the earliest constitution, belonged to the king. The patriciate was, by this time, a small body in the state, and all of its members were to be found in the *nobilitas* as well. The first one of a plebeian family to hold a curule office was called a *novus homo*, and his success insured the nobility of all his direct descendants. From the beginning efforts were made to limit the number of families from which representatives were chosen for high positions in the state, and to cultivate a class spirit among those who had been thus honored. One of the consuls, for example, was by law always a plebeian, but there was nothing to prevent the office from going in succession to each of half a dozen brothers. The *Fasti*, for the period after the Licinian laws were enacted, bear witness to the success of these efforts. Year after year the same *cognomina* appear constantly in the lists of curule magistrates. By law, almost the only privilege secured to the *nobilitas* was the *jus imaginum*. This was the right to place in the *atrium* of one's house the wax images of illustrious ancestors, and to carry them in the funeral processions by which the family's dead were honored. Practically, however, as has been said, the administration of the government soon passed entirely into the hands of the *nobilitas*.

2. **The Constitution of the Senate.**—It will be necessary to discuss at some length several points before it will be clearly shown how the *no-*

*bilitas* gained this power. But we give the clew to the explanation when we say that its organ in the management of affairs was the senate. When the consul succeeded to the functions of the king at the founding of the republic, the selection of senators was one of his duties. In 435 B. C., this function, along with others, was transferred to the censorship, then first established. The control which the censors got in this way over the organization of the senate, as well as over the popular assemblies, made this position the most powerful in the state, and therefore the most coveted. The extent and consequences of their power over the popular assemblies will be discussed in another connection, but, in the choice of members of the senate, they were limited by a law which secured to every curule officer a seat in the senate on the expiration of his magistracy. The censors, furthermore, were not allowed to set aside this law in any case without publishing a justification of their course, based on the proved unfitness of the candidate for the position. The number of former incumbents of curule offices was, of course, insufficient to fill the vacancies which occurred, and the censors were unrestricted in the selection of the rest. Being nobles themselves almost without exception, they naturally picked out for these places, first, prominent young nobles who had not yet held a curule office; sometimes they honored a soldier who had distinguished himself on the battle-field; and often they were actuated in their choice by nothing better than partiality or personal friendship. In the meetings of the senate, priority of voting belonged to the ex-consuls, who formed a class by themselves, and were called *consulares*. After them the ex-prætors or *prætorii* voted; then the *ædilicii*, or ex-curule ædiles; and, finally, the *pedarii*, or those who had not held any curule office. It will be remembered that, when the senate was reorganized at the beginning of the republic, the *conscripti*, who were given votes, were not allowed to debate. In the same way, now, the right of speaking was reserved exclusively to the first three of the classes just enumerated.

3. **The Theoretical Functions of the Senate.**—If we should search the statute-books of the Romans in order to learn what this body had to do with the government of the state, it would seem as though a seat in the senate was a sort of empty honor, worth striving for because of its dignity, but for no other reason. By law, the only powers of the senate were the *patrum auctoritas*, by which is meant the right of confirming a law or election made in one of the popular assemblies, and the right of administering an *interregnum* when there chanced to be a lapse in the regular order of succession to the consulship. No statute can be found which enlarged the sphere of the senate beyond these original limits; and more than that, these powers belonged as exclusively to the patrician members down to the time of the empire as they had at the outset. No senator, however noble, was at all concerned with either of these things unless he was of patrician blood, but this made no

difference to him because these functions were of no value. An *interregnum* was a very remote possibility in a state where the consul held over by law until his successor was appointed; and at least as early as 339 B. C. it was provided in the same way that the senate must ratify in advance all the laws and *plebiscita* of the popular assemblies. A little later a similar preliminary indorsement was required of it in the case of elections also, until these original and traditional powers were nothing but empty formalities which were observed simply because the Romans' respect for the past forbade their disregarding them. The senate was a nullity in the state, therefore, on this side, at the time of the second Punic war. But from another side, as we shall presently show, its sphere had grown and extended until all the legislative and executive business of the government was transacted at its dictation. This, however, was entirely at variance with the theory of the constitution, which made the popular assemblies the ultimate source of all authority in the state.

4. **The Popular Assemblies enumerated.** —To repeat in a consecutive way what has been given in the preceding chapter, there were at this time four of these popular assemblies which exercised real or nominal legislative functions. In the order of their institution, as far as this can be learned, they were the *comitia curiata*, the *comitia centuriata*, the *concilium tributum plebis* or plebeian assembly of the tribes, and the *comitia tributa*, in which both patricians and plebeians had votes.

The *comitia curiata* had primitively been a purely patrician organization, but after a reform, conjectured to have been made about the end of the regal period, the plebeians had gained admission to it. This change made it a democratic body, in which the unit was the *curia*. In historical times, however, it met only to sanction certain forms of adoption or the restoration of a returned exile to his clan, and to confer the *imperium* on the magistrates. But this in reality amounted to little, because the grant of the *imperium* was never refused, and so few of the citizens attended the meetings that thirty lictors usually represented the thirty *curiæ* and transacted business for them. All the real power enjoyed by the people was exercised in the *comitia centuriata*, in the separate plebeian assembly, or in the patricio-plebeian *comitia tributa*. The organization of all these bodies at the time under consideration was dependent on the division of the people into tribes. It is necessary at this point, therefore, to discuss somewhat further the nature of a tribe.

5. **The Composition of a Tribe.**—We have seen that the four city tribes were dated by the Romans from the time of Servius Tullius, that is, from very remote antiquity. The seventeen country tribes took their names from the principal clans, and were believed to be only a little younger. Others were from time to time created in the territory earliest conquered, until the number thirty-five was reached. This, as already stated, was never exceeded. All these tribes were primarily nothing but territorial divisions. All the land-holders in a

certain district were, from that fact, members of the same tribe, and at first it was possible for a man to change his tribe by changing his residence. Afterward, however, when the number of tribes had nearly reached its maximum limit, this was altered. The inhabitants of whole cities were now assigned, once for all, to a particular tribe. A man's position in a tribe ceased in this way to be dependent on the situation of his estate, and became personal and hereditary. It still continued necessary for him to be a freeholder in order to enjoy membership in a tribe; but if he gave up his farm near Tusculum, for example, and secured another near Formiæ, he and his descendants none the less belonged to the Papirian tribe along with the rest of the people of Tusculum who had not changed their residence. This reform, too, was accompanied by efforts to somehow include in the tribal organization those who were not freeholders, in order that they might be liable to active service in the army. For this purpose, in 312 B. C., Appius Claudius placed their names in the list of voters, allowing them to select which of the tribes they would be numbered in. This secured them the right of suffrage, but at the same time imposed on them the various burdens of citizenship. A few years afterward, Fabius Rullianus assigned them all to the four city tribes, and this arrangement was finally established as the rule.

6. **The Censors' Control over the Tribes.** —Claudius and Fabius had the authority to make these innovations, because at the time they were

censors, and the censors had entire control over the organization of the tribes. This gained them great power, and the means of giving positive effect to their jurisdiction over the morals of the common citizens. At first, by way of punishment, they could exclude a man altogether from the tribes; and, after the changes just detailed had been made, they could take him out of his proper tribe and put him in one of the enormous city tribes. His individual vote would count for little here in determining the vote of the tribe. His political influence would thus be made very small in those assemblies which were based on the tribal arrangement. These were from the outset, of course, the *concilium tributum plebis* and the *comitia tributa*, and, after a reform of uncertain date, the *comitia centuriata* also. The details of this reform are much too obscure to be considered here, but enough must be said to show that the *comitia centuriata* was not the same organization all through the history of the republic. For one thing it was now provided that a fixed number of centuries should be taken from each tribe. The arrangement of the centuries into classes on the basis of age and wealth was thenceforth made within each tribe separately, and the marshaling of all the citizens in a body for this purpose abandoned. The same number of votes was also given to each of the five classes at this time. This was an important change in a democratic direction. There had been no class distinction of any kind in the assemblies of the tribes from the first, but in the *comitia centuriata* the richer men, though far less numerous, had possessed a controlling voice. After this reform, however, the votes of the knights, the first class and the second class combined, did not make a majority, but those of the third class had yet to be taken before a decision could be reached. Finally, under the original constitution of the assembly, the *equites* had enjoyed the privilege of voting first on any measure which came before it. The *equites* at this period consisted of senators and young nobles of wealth, who could always be relied on to look out for the interests of the *nobilitas*. Their having this priority, therefore, secured a great advantage for the aristocracy, because the cue was often given to all the centuries which followed by the way in which they treated a proposition. The right was now, however, taken from them and assigned to a century chosen by lot from the first class, and called the *centuria prærogativa*.

7. **The Theoretical Powers of the Popular Assemblies.**—To continue our summary, these three assemblies—that is, the *comitia centuriata*, the *concilium tributum plebis*, and the *comitia tributa*—had all the right of making laws. The *comitia centuriata* was, at first, the only legislative body, and continued for some time to be the principal one. The *concilium plebis* seems to have obtained the full right of independent legislation by the Hortensian law, passed about 287 B. C. The activity of the patricio-plebeian *comitia tributa* dates from the time of the fall of the decemvirs, when the quæstors were made elective magistrates. These were from the beginning chosen by the whole people assembled, not by

centuries, but by tribes. Laws began also to be brought before this assembly soon after the institution of the prætorship. In later times, the more important laws were far more commonly passed in one or the other assembly of the tribes than in the *comitia centuriata*, because they could be got together with fewer and less burdensome formalities.

The election of the higher magistrates (the consuls, prætors, and censors) remained the sole right of the centuriate assembly, while the inferior officers (the quæstors and curule ædiles) were selected by the tribes. The election of the plebeian magistrates (the tribunes and plebeian ædiles) took place, of course, in the plebeian assembly.

The declaration of an offensive war was, at all times, made only by the *comitia centuriata*, but it was the *comitia tributa* which was consulted about concluding a peace or forming an alliance when these things were referred by the consuls to the people.

If one sentenced to capital punishment took exception to the judgment of the magistrate, his appeal had to go, according to the laws of the Twelve Tables, to the *comitia centuriata*. But, if it were merely a fine which was involved, an appeal in such case commonly went to one of the assemblies of the tribes. If the tribunes or plebeian ædile had imposed the fine, the appeal was taken to the plebeian assembly; and, otherwise, to the full assembly of the whole people.

8. **The Magistrates' Control over the Popular Assemblies.**—This exhibit of the constitution and powers of the popular assemblies

shows the truth of the statement, made at the beginning of the chapter, that the government of Rome, at the time of the second Punic war, was in theory a democracy. Every man, freeholder and non-freeholder, could vote in all the legislative bodies, and the vote of one man counted, in general, for as much as that of another, except so far as the size of his tribe made a difference. Besides this, the executive officers, being chosen for brief periods by the people, were, it would seem, simply their representatives, while the senate's legal power of veto was only a formality. The accuracy of all this, however, as a statement of the theory of the government, is not at all inconsistent with the fact that the real power belonged entirely to the *nobilitas*. Part of the explanation is to be found in the peculiar power of a magistrate in a Roman popular assembly. His position is not to be thought of as like that of a chairman in one of our town-meetings. The Roman magistrate called and adjourned the assembly as he pleased. He framed the proposal which he laid before the people according to his own ideas, and simply allowed them to indorse or reject it as it stood. The assembly had no right of free debate and no power of amendment. In general, particularly after the Roman territory became so extended that it was quite impossible for all the citizens to gather in the capital, the presiding magistrate seems to have had the assembly pretty completely in his own hand. Even in an election, which was the principal manifestation of actual power, the consuls, who always presided, except in the case of the election of tribunes, could exert very great influence on the result. They could even go so far in this direction as to refuse to receive votes for a candidate who was obnoxious to them. The powers of the assemblies are, in this light, to be regarded as in the main practically powers of the magistrates, who had the right of calling them together. Now, the *jus agendi cum populo*, the right of calling together the whole people, and with them passing resolutions binding on the whole community, belonged at first to the king, and, under the republican constitution, to the consul, prætor, dictator, and *magister equitum*, as, also, during the period of their existence, to the decemvirs and the consular tribunes. The *jus agendi cum plebe*, which was just as effective, belonged to the tribunes of the people. The *concilium plebis* was, therefore, the legislative organ of the tribunes. The *comitia centuriata* was regularly made use of by the consuls only, though probably the prætor had the theoretical right of summoning it. The *comitia tributa* of the whole people, on the other hand, was employed freely as machinery for this purpose by either consuls or prætors.

9. **The Senate's Control over the Magistrates.**—The magistrates, in this way, exercised a control over the popular assemblies which was quite contrary to the theory of the constitution, but they, in their turn, were subject to the power of the senate, which, we have seen, was the organ of the *nobilitas*. It will be remembered that along with the rights of the senators, even under the regal

constitution, there was put upon them the duty of advising the king whenever he saw fit to consult them. It was for this purpose that the *conscripti* had originally been called in to assist the *patres*, and the patrician and plebeian members of the senate stood on an equality in the discharge of this duty. From so simple a beginning were developed the enormous powers which the body subsequently held. As the *pater familias*, before he put a son to death, was expected to get the advice of a council composed of his fellow-clansmen (*gentiles*), so the king was expected, in all important matters, to consult his council of experienced old men. In the time of the republic no change was made by law in the principle that the senate should give advice to the magistrate only when asked for it. But, as every man who had held a curule office gained from this fact a seat in the senate, the senate came to be composed, by a sort of indirect election, of the best men in the state. Its leaders were nobles who had been trained from boyhood in the principles of government. They had all had the benefit of experience in administration. Every great general, all the men who had acquaintance with foreign countries from having lived in them as governors or embassadors, every wise statesman and lawyer —all these were sure to be found on the benches of the senate.

10. **The Senate's Control over the Magistrates** (*continued*).—The moral influence of such a body's opinion was irresistible. The consuls who held office only for a year, and therefore had no

time to build up a personal ascendency, found it impossible to withstand such a close corporation whose members held office for life. And so, although strictly, according to law, the magistrate was under no compulsion to summon the senate nor to follow its advice when he had obtained it, it became thoroughly understood that, as a matter of fact, the senate was to be carefully consulted and implicitly obeyed. Theoretically it was not a legislative body. The popular assemblies alone had the power to pass laws. But actually the assemblies were under the control of the magistrates, and the magistrates were nothing more than the commissioners of the senate. No magistrate would bring a law before the people without first asking the senate's advice. There every bill was open to free debate, and the vote which was there taken settled the question of its passage. If the senate decided against a measure, the magistrate would not propose it to the people. If, on the other hand, the senate favored a law, out of the many officers who had the *jus agendi cum populo*, or the equally effective *jus agendi cum plebe*, it was not hard to find one who would carry it through some one of the popular assemblies. In this way practically all the legislating in the Roman state was done by the senate at the time of the second Punic war.

11. **The Senate's Executive Power.**—In the matter of administration, the senate maintained the chief power in two ways. In the internal government of the city, it relied mainly on the fact that it had control of the state's finances. This was the

result of a gradual usurpation on its part, but, when perfected, the consul was the only officer who could draw money from the treasury without its consent. And there was a limitation on his power in this direction, because this right belonged to him only when within the city in the discharge of civil functions. But here the institution of offices like the censorship and ædileship had transferred all the duties which involved large expenditures to magistrates who were under the control of the senate. In foreign affairs, the senate got very wide powers in the course of time, from the right which it had of deciding whether war should be declared or not. By sanctioning or refusing an unusual levy, by assigning to a consul his field of operations, or by sending instructions to the commander, it directed the conduct of the war. In times of emergency it could supersede the consuls by directing them to appoint a dictator. This was in spite of the fact that the right of appointment legally belonged to the consuls solely, for the consuls, under the force of custom, felt themselves morally bound to submit in this as in other matters to the body from which many of them were selected for the consulship, and in which they would all be enrolled at the expiration of their term. Finally, it came within the sphere of the senate, thus enlarged, to make treaties of peace or alliance, to receive embassadors from foreign states, and to send them, and, when Rome began to form provinces out of the countries she conquered, to devise governments and provide governors for them.

12. **The Rule of the Nobilitas.**—It is very

obvious from all this that, at the best period of Roman history, the government had altered very materially from its original pattern. At the outset, it had consisted of three co-ordinate parts—the chief magistrate, who executed what the old men advised and the populace ordered. At the point which we have reached, one of these three departments ruled the state as completely as the House of Commons in England to-day exercises the power which it theoretically shares with the crown and the House of Lords. It was under the disinterested and able administration of the *nobilitas*, through its organ, the senate, that Rome advanced in greatness until all the countries which bordered on the Mediterranean came under her sway. The wisdom and skill of the senate knit together the empire, thus formed, with bonds which were flexible enough to be just and yet strong enough to secure its integrity. In the most trying hours of Roman history, as when Hannibal was advancing on the walls of the city, it was the senate which devised the means of rescue, just as in the day of triumph the senate rewarded the victorious general with the right to lead the triumphal procession up the Capitoline Hill. With the lapse of years, however, the problem of government increased in difficulty, and the character of the men who had to solve it suffered in the moral decay which came over the Romans in the century before the empire. Italian agriculture was crushed by the strength of foreign competition. Capital, assuming enormous dimensions, blocked commerce and traffic of every kind against the small dealer. The dignity of labor perished because all the trades were filled with slaves, and the city populace became a rabble living on politics and war. When the senate, which was itself composed of a different class of men from that which had won for it its fame, found itself unequal to the task of satisfying the needs of this clamorous throng, and, at the same time, of directing the concerns of the empire, the rule of the *nobilitas* came to an end.

13. **The Transition to the Empire.**—Then began the irresponsible government of the plebeian tribuneship, which, after a hundred years of interrupted ascendency, made the depotism of the emperors a welcome relief. There are three stages in the history of the tribunate. At first it was the chief instrument of the plebeians in their struggle for equal rights. During the best period of Roman history it was composed chiefly of plebeian nobles, and was the main reliance of the *nobilitas*. The tribunes had, equally with the consuls and prætors, the *jus referendi ad senatum*, or the right of calling the senate together and laying matters before it, and the senate frequently took advantage of their loyalty to have them bring before it subjects on which it desired to vote. From the time of the Gracchi, however, with some exceptions, as when the constitution of Sulla restored the government to the senate, the tribunes used their immense power in reckless violation of even the slight restraints which custom had put upon it. In the period before the second Punic war, there are occasional instances when the popular assemblies under the leadership

of a tribune took upon their shoulders administrative measures to the exclusion of the senate. So, for example, in 232 B. C., at the instigation of Gaius Flaminius, although the senate opposed it, the people passed an agrarian law, dividing among themselves certain lands in Gaul which had been acquired in war. Such interferences, however, were extraordinary, and regarded as infringements of the constitution of the state. When they became common, the republic came to an end. The government of the senate, in the last years of its power, has received the just censure of those who are capable of criticising it. But the rule of the tribunes, who voiced the caprice of the city rabble, was but little better than anarchy. The ultimate outcome was the establishment of the empire. Rome thus accomplished the circle through which, in theory, all governments tend to pass—monarchy, aristocracy, democracy, anarchy—and began the round again.

THE END.

# PRIMERS
## IN SCIENCE, HISTORY, AND LITERATURE.
18mo. Flexible cloth, 45 cents each.

### SCIENCE PRIMERS.
Edited by Professors HUXLEY, ROSCOE, and BALFOUR STEWART.

Introductory. Prof. T. H. Huxley, F. R. S.
Chemistry. Prof. H. E. Roscoe, F. R. S.
Physics. Prof. Balfour Stewart, F. R. S.
Physical Geography. Prof. A. Geikie, F. R. S.
Geology. Prof. A. Geikie, F. R. S.
Physiology. M. Foster, M. D., F. R. S.
Hygiene. R. S. Tracy.
Astronomy. J. N. Lockyer, F. R. S.
Botany. Sir J. D. Hooker, F.R.S.
Logic. Prof. W. S. Jevons, F.R.S.
Inventional Geometry. W. G. Spencer.
Pianoforte. Franklin Taylor.
Political Economy. Prof. W. S. Jevons, F. R. S.
Natural Resources of the United States. J. H. Patton, A. M.

### HISTORY PRIMERS.
Edited by J. R. GREEN, M. A., Examiner in the School of Modern History at Oxford.

Greece. C. A. Fyffe, M. A.
Rome. M. Creighton, M. A.
Europe. E. A. Freeman, D. C. L.
Old Greek Life. J. P. Mahaffy, M. A.
Roman Antiquities. Prof. A. S. Wilkins.
Geography. George Grove, F. R. G. S.
France. Charlotte M. Yonge.
Mediæval Civilization. Prof. G. B. Adams.
Roman Constitution. Ambrose Tighe.

### LITERATURE PRIMERS.
Edited by J. R. GREEN, M. A.

English Grammar. R. Morris, LL. D.
English Literature. Rev. Stopford A. Brooke, M. A.
Philology. J. Peile, M. A.
Classical Geography. M. F. Tozer.
Shakespeare. Prof. E. Dowden.
Studies in Bryant. J. Alden.
Greek Literature. Prof. R. C. Jebb.
English Grammar Exercises. R. Morris, LL. D., and H. C. Bowen, M. A.
Homer. Right Hon. W. E. Gladstone.
English Composition. Prof. J. Nichol.

The object of these primers is to convey information in such a manner as to make it both intelligible and interesting to very young pupils, and so to discipline their minds as to incline them to more systematic after-studies. The woodcuts which illustrate them embellish and explain the text at the same time.

New York: D. APPLETON & CO., 1, 3, & 5 Bond Street.

www.ingramcontent.com/pod-product-compliance
Lightning Source LLC
Chambersburg PA
CBHW020059170426
43199CB00009B/339